Hannibal the Carthaginian

Hannibal the Carthaginian

Makers of History Series

Jacob Abbott

Cedar Lake Classics

Copyright © 2023 by Cedar Lake Classics

This is an annotated edition of a public domain work.

CONTENTS

PREFACE vii

1. The First Punic War 1
2. Hannibal Saguntum 13
3. Opening of the Second Punic War 23
4. The Passage of the Rhone 33
5. Hannibal Crosses the Alps 44
6. Hannibal in the North of Italy 63
7. The Apennines 73
8. The Dictator Fabius 84
9. The Battle of Cannæ 96
10. Scipio 107
11. Hannibal a Fugitive and an Exile 123
12. The Destruction of Carthage 137

CONTENTS

ABOUT JACOB ABBOTT **157**
BIOGRAPHIES ABBOTT WROTE **159**

PREFACE

THE author of this series has made it his special object to confine himself very strictly, even in the most minute details which he records, to historic truth. The narratives are not tales founded upon history, but history itself, without any embellishment or any deviations from the strict truth, so far as it can now be discovered by an attentive examination of the annals written at the time when the events themselves occurred.

In writing the narratives, the author has endeavored to avail himself of the best sources of information which this country affords; and though, of course, there must be in these volumes, as in all historical narratives, more or less of imperfection and error, there is no intentional embellishment.

Nothing is stated, not even the most minute and apparently imaginary details, without what was deemed good historical authority. The readers, therefore, may rely upon the record as the truth, and nothing but the truth, so far as honest purpose and a careful examination has been effectual in ascertaining it.

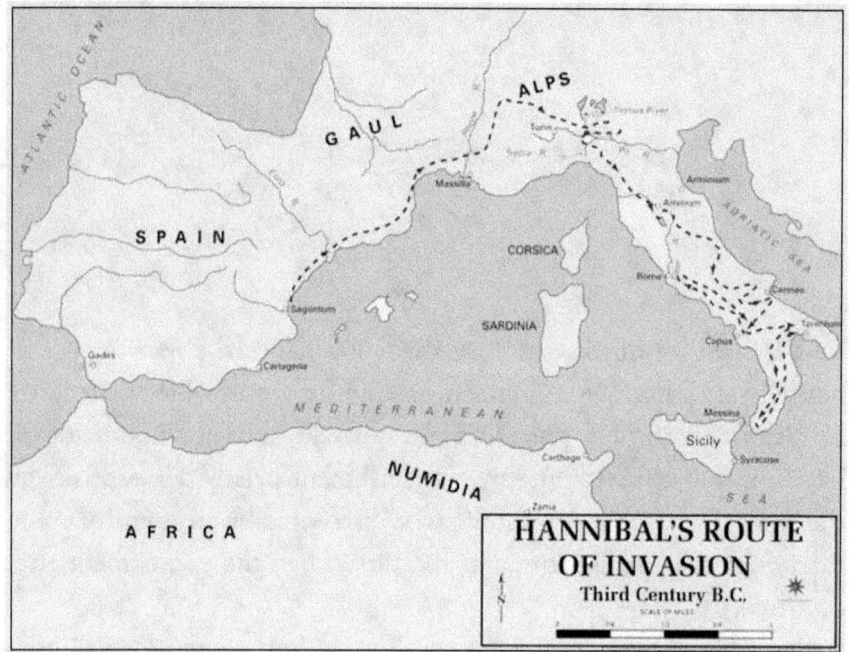

1

The First Punic War

HANNIBAL was a Carthaginian general. He acquired his great distinction as a warrior by his desperate contests with the Romans. Rome and Carthage grew up together on opposite sides of the Mediterranean Sea. For about a hundred years they waged against each other most dreadful wars. There were three of these wars. Rome was successful in the end, and Carthage was entirely destroyed.

There was no real cause for any disagreement between these two nations. Their hostility to each other was mere rivalry and spontaneous hate. They spoke a different language; they had a different origin; and they lived on opposite sides of the same sea. So they hated and devoured each other.

Those who have read the history of Alexander the Great, in this series, will recollect the difficulty he experienced in besieging and subduing Tyre, a great maritime city, situated about two miles from the shore, on the eastern coast of the Mediterranean Sea. Carthage was originally founded by a colony from this city of Tyre, and it soon became a great commercial and maritime power like its mother. The Carthaginians built ships, and with them explored all parts of the Mediterranean Sea. They visited all the nations on these coasts, purchased the commodities they had to sell, carried them to other nations, and sold them at great advances. They soon began to grow rich and powerful. They hired soldiers to fight their battles, and began to take possession of the islands of the Mediterranean, and, in some instances, of points on the main land.

For example, in Spain: some of their ships, going there, found that the natives had silver and gold, which they obtained from veins of ore near the surface of the ground. At first the Carthaginians obtained this gold and silver by selling the natives commodities of various kinds, which they had procured in other countries; paying, of course, to the producers only a very small price compared with what they required the Spaniards to pay them. Finally, they took possession of that part of Spain where the mines were situated, and worked the mines themselves. They dug deeper; they employed skillful engineers to make pumps to raise the water, which always accumulates in mines, and prevents their being worked to any great depth unless the miners have a considerable degree of scientific and mechanical skill. They founded a city here, which they called New Carthage—Nova Carthago. They fortified and garrisoned this city, and made it the center of their operations in Spain. This city is called Carthagena to this day.

Thus the Carthaginians did every thing by power of money. They extended their operations in every direction, each new extension bringing in new treasures, and increasing their means of extending them more. They had, besides the merchant vessels which belonged to private individuals, great ships of war belonging to the state. These vessels were called galleys, and were rowed by oarsmen, tier above tier, there being sometimes four and five banks of oars. They had armies, too, drawn from different countries, in various troops, according as different nations excelled in the different modes of warfare. For instance, the Numidians, whose country extended in the neighborhood of Carthage, on the African coast, were famous for their horsemen. There were great plains in Numidia, and good grazing, and it was, consequently, one of those countries in which horses and horsemen naturally thrive. On the other hand, the natives of the Balearic Isles, now called Majorca, Minorca, and Ivica, were famous for their skill as slingers. So the Carthaginians, in making up their forces, would hire bodies of cavalry in

Numidia, and of slingers in the Balearic Isles; and, for reasons analogous, they got excellent infantry in Spain.

The tendency of the various nations to adopt and cultivate different modes of warfare was far greater in those ancient times than now. The Balearic Isles, in fact, received their name from the Greek word ballein, which means to throw with a sling. The youth there were trained to perfection in the use of this weapon from a very early age. It is said that mothers used to practice the plan of putting the bread for their boys' breakfast on the branches of trees, high above their heads, and not allow them to have their food to eat until they could bring it down with a stone thrown from a sling.

Thus the Carthaginian power became greatly extended. The whole government, however was exercised by a small body of wealthy and aristocratic families at home. It was very much such a government as that of England is at the present day, only the aristocracy of England is based on ancient birth and landed property, whereas in Carthage it depended on commercial greatness, combined, it is true, with hereditary family distinction. The aristocracy of Carthage controlled and governed every thing. None but its own sons could ordinarily obtain office or power. The great mass of inhabitants were kept in a state of servitude and vassalage. This state of things operated then, as it does now in England, very unjustly and hardly for those who were thus debased; but the result was—and in this respect the analogy with England still holds good—that a very efficient and energetic government was created. The government of an oligarchy makes sometimes a very rich and powerful state, but a discontented and unhappy people.

Let the reader now turn to the map and find the place of Carthage upon it. Let him imagine a great and rich city there, with piers, and docks, and extensive warehouses for the commerce, and temples, and public edifices of splendid architecture, for the religious and civil service of the state, and elegant mansions and palaces for the wealthy aristocracy, and walls and towers for the defense of the whole. Let him then imagine a back country, extending for some hundred miles into the interior of Africa, fertile and highly cultivated, producing great stores of corn, and wine, and rich fruits of every description. Let him then look at the islands of Sicily, of Corsica, and Sardinia, and the Baleares, and conceive of them as rich and prosperous countries, and all under the Carthaginian rule. Look, also, at the coast of Spain; see, in imagination, the city of Carthagena, with its fortifications, and its army, and the gold and silver mines, with thousands and thousands of slaves toiling in them. Imagine fleets of ships going continually along the shores of the Mediterranean, from country to country, cruising back and forth to Tyre, to Cyprus, to Egypt, to Sicily, to Spain, carrying corn, and flax, and purple dyes, and spices, and perfumes, and precious stones, and ropes, and sails for ships, and gold and silver, and then periodically returning to Carthage, to add the profits they had made to the vast treasures of wealth already accumulated there. Let the reader imagine all this with the map before him, so as to have a distinct conception of the geographical relations of the localities, and he will have a pretty correct idea of the Carthaginian power at the time it commenced its dreadful conflicts with Rome.

Rome itself was very differently situated. Rome had been built by some wanderers from Troy, and it grew, for a long time, silently and slowly, by a sort of internal principle of life and energy. One region after another of the Italian peninsula was merged in the Roman state. They formed a population which was, in the main, stationary and agricultural. They tilled the fields; they hunted the wild beasts; they raised great flocks and herds. They seem to have been a race—a sort of variety of the human species—possessed of a very refined and superior organization, which, in its development, gave rise to a character of firmness, energy, and force, both of body and mind, which has justly excited the admiration of mankind. The Carthaginians had sagacity—the Romans called it cunning—and activity, enterprise and wealth. Their rivals, on the other hand, were characterized by genius, courage, and strength, giving rise to a certain calm and indomitable resolution and energy, which has since, in every age, been strongly associated, in the minds of men, with the very word Roman.

The progress of nations was much more slow in ancient days than now, and these two rival empires continued their gradual growth and extension, each on its own side of the great sea which divided them, for five hundred years, before they came into collision. At last, however, the collision came. It originated in the following way:

By looking at the map, the reader will see that the island of Sicily is separated from the main land by a narrow strait called the Strait of Messina. This strait derives its name from the town of Messina, which is situated upon it, on the Sicilian side. Opposite Messina, on the Italian side, there was a town named Rhegium. Now it happened that both these towns had been taken possession of by lawless bodies of soldiery. The Romans came and delivered Rhegium, and punished the soldiers who had seized it very severely. The Sicilian authorities advanced to the deliverance of Messina. The troops there, finding themselves thus threatened, sent to the Romans to say that if they, the Romans, would come and protect them, they would deliver Messina into their hands.

The question, what answer to give to this application, was brought before the Roman senate, and caused them great perplexity. It seemed very inconsistent to take sides with the rebels of Messina, when they had punished so severely those of Rhegium. Still the Romans had been, for a long time, becoming very jealous of the growth and extension of the Carthaginian power. Here was an opportunity of meeting and resisting it. The Sicilian authorities were about calling for direct aid from Carthage to recover the city, and the affair would probably result in establishing a large body of Carthaginian troops within sight of the Italian shore, and at a point where it would be easy for them to make hostile incursions into the Roman territories. In a word, it was a case of what is called political necessity; that is to say, a case in which the interests of one of the parties in a contest were so strong that all considerations of justice, consistency, and honor are to be sacrificed to the promotion of them. Instances of this kind of political necessity occur very frequently in the management of public affairs in all ages of the world.

The contest for Messina was, after all, however, considered by the Romans merely as a pretext, or rather as an occasion, for commencing the struggle which they had long been desirous of entering upon. They evinced their characteristic energy and greatness in the plan which they adopted at the outset. They knew very well that the power of Carthage rested mainly on her command of the seas, and that they could not hope successfully to cope with her till they could meet and conquer her on her own element. In the mean time, however, they had not a single ship and not a single sailor, while the Mediterranean was covered with Carthaginian ships and seamen. Not at all daunted by this prodigious inequality, the Romans resolved to begin at once the work of creating for themselves a naval power.

The preparations consumed some time; for the Romans had not only to build the ships, they had first to learn how to build them. They took their first lesson from a Carthaginian galley which was cast away in a storm upon the coast of Italy. They seized this galley, collected their carpenters to examine it, and set woodmen at work to fell trees and collect materials for imitating it. The carpenters studied their model very carefully, measured the dimensions of every part, and observed the manner in which the various parts were connected and secured together. The heavy shocks which vessels are exposed to from the waves makes it necessary to secure great strength in the construction of them; and, though the ships of the ancients were very small and imperfect compared with the men-of-war of the present day, still it is surprising that the Romans could succeed at all in such a sudden and hasty attempt at building them.

They did, however, succeed. While the ships were building, officers appointed for the purpose were training men, on shore, to the art of rowing them. Benches, like the seats which the oarsman would occupy in the ships, were arranged on the ground, and the intended seamen were drilled every day in the movements and action of rowers. The result was, that in a few months after the building of the ships was commenced, the Romans had a fleet of one hundred galleys of five banks of oars ready. They remained in harbor with them for some time, to give the oarsmen the opportunity to see whether they could row on the water as well as on the land, and then boldly put to sea to meet the Carthaginians.

There was one part of the arrangements made by the Romans in preparing their fleets which was strikingly characteristic of the determined resolution which marked all their conduct. They constructed machines containing grappling irons, which they mounted on the prows of their vessels. These engines were so contrived, that the moment one of the ships containing them should encounter a vessel of the enemy, the grappling irons would fall upon the deck of the latter, and hold the two firmly together, so as to prevent the possibility of either escaping from the other. The idea that they themselves should have any wish to withdraw from the encounter seemed entirely out of the question. Their only fear was that the Carthaginian seamen would employ their superior skill and experience in naval maneuvers in making their escape. Mankind have always regarded the action of the Romans, in this case, as one of the most striking examples of military courage and resolution which the history of war has ever recorded. An army of landsmen come down to the sea-shore, and, without scarcely having ever seen a ship, undertake to build a fleet, and go out to attack a power whose navies covered the sea, and made her the sole and acknowledged mistress of it. They seize a wrecked galley of their enemies for their model; they build a hundred vessels like it: they practice maneuvers for a short time in port; and then go forth to meet the fleets of their powerful enemy, with grappling machines to hold them, fearing nothing but the possibility of their escape.

The result was as might have been expected. The Romans captured, sunk, destroyed, or dispersed the Carthaginian fleet which was brought to oppose them. They took the prows of the ships which they captured and conveyed them to Rome, and built what is called a rostral pillar of them. A rostral pillar is a column ornamented with such beaks or prows, which were, in the Roman language, called rostra. This column was nearly destroyed by lightning about fifty years afterward, but it was repaired and rebuilt again, and it stood then for many centuries, a very striking and appropriate monument of this extraordinary naval victory. The Roman commander in this case was the consul Duilius. The rostral column was erected in honor of him. In digging among the ruins of Rome, there was found what was supposed to be the remains of this column, about three hundred years ago.

The Romans now prepared to carry the war into Africa itself. Of course it was easy, after their victory over the Carthaginian fleet, to transport troops across the sea to the Carthaginian shore. The Roman commonwealth was governed at this time by a senate, who made the laws, and by two supreme executive officers, called consuls. They thought it was safer to have two chief magistrates than one, as each of the two would naturally be a check upon the other. The result was, however, that mutual jealousy involved them often in disputes and quarrels. It is thought better, in modern times, to have but one chief magistrate in the state, and to provide other modes to put a check upon any disposition he might evince to abuse his powers.

The Roman consuls, in time of war, took command of the armies. The name of the consul upon whom it devolved to carry on the war with the Carthaginians, after this first great victory, was Regulus, and his name has been celebrated in every age, on account of his extraordinary adventures in this campaign, and his untimely fate. How far the story is strictly true it is now impossible to ascertain, but the following is the story, as the Roman historians relate it:

At the time when Regulus was elected consul he was a plain man, living simply on his farm, maintaining himself by his own industry, and evincing no ambition or pride. His fellow-citizens, however, observed those qualities of mind in him which they were accustomed to admire, and made him consul. He left the city and took command of the army. He enlarged the fleet to more than three hundred vessels. He put one hundred and forty thousand men on board and sailed for Africa. One or two years had been spent in making these preparations, which time the Carthaginians had improved in building new ships; so that, when the Romans set sail, and were moving along the coast of Sicily, they soon came in sight of a larger Carthaginian fleet assembled to oppose them. Regulus advanced to the contest. The Carthaginian fleet was beaten as before. The ships which were not captured or destroyed made their escape in all directions, and Regulus went on, without further opposition, and landed his forces on the Carthaginian shore. He encamped as soon as he landed, and sent back word to the Roman senate asking what was next to be done.

The senate, considering that the great difficulty and danger, viz., that of repulsing the Carthaginian fleet, was now past, ordered Regulus to send home nearly all the ships and a very large part of the army, and with the rest to commence his march toward Carthage. Regulus obeyed: he sent home the troops which had been ordered home, and with the rest began to advance upon the city.

Just at this time, however, news came out to him that the farmer who had had the care of his land at home had died, and that his little farm, on which rested his sole reliance for the support of his family, was going to ruin. Regulus accordingly sent to the senate, asking them to place some one else in command of the army, and to allow him to resign his office, that he might go home and take care of his wife and children. The senate sent back orders that he should go on with his campaign, and promised to provide support for his family, and to see that some one was appointed to take care of his land. This story is thought to illustrate the extreme simplicity and plainness of all the habits of life among the Romans in those days. It certainly does so, if it is true. It is, however, very extraordinary, that a man who was intrusted, by such a commonwealth, with the command of a fleet of a hundred and thirty vessels, and an army of a hundred and forty thousand men, should have a family at home dependent for subsistence on the hired cultivation of seven acres of land. Still, such is the story.

Regulus advanced toward Carthage, conquering as he came. The Carthaginians were beaten in one field after another, and were reduced, in fact, to the last extremity, when an occurrence took place which turned the scale. This was the arrival of a large body of troops from Greece, with a Grecian general at their head. These were troops which the Carthaginians had hired to fight for them, as was the case with the rest of the army. But these were Greeks, and the Greeks were of the same race, and possessed the same qualities, as the Romans. The newly-arrived Grecian general evinced at once such military superiority, that the Carthaginians gave him the supreme command. He marshaled the army, accordingly, for battle. He had a hundred elephants in the van. They were trained to rush forward and trample down the enemy. He had the Greek phalanx in the center, which was a close, compact body of many thousand troops, bristling with long, iron-pointed spears, with which the men pressed forward, bearing every thing before them. Regulus was, in a word, ready to meet Carthaginians, but he was not prepared to encounter Greeks. His army was put to flight, and he was taken prisoner. Nothing could exceed the excitement and exultation in the city when they saw Regulus, and five hundred other Roman soldiers, brought captive in. A few days before, they had been in consternation at the imminent danger of his coming in as a ruthless and vindictive conqueror.

The Roman senate were not discouraged by this disaster. They fitted out new armies, and the war went on, Regulus being kept all the time at Carthage as a close prisoner. At last the Carthaginians authorized him to go to Rome as a sort of commissioner, to propose to the Romans to exchange prisoners and to make peace. They exacted from him a solemn promise that if he was unsuccessful he would return. The Romans had taken many of the Carthaginians prisoners in their naval combats, and held them captive at Rome. It is customary, in such cases, for the belligerent nations to make an exchange, and restore the captives on both sides to their friends and home. It was such an exchange of prisoners as this which Regulus was to propose.

When Regulus reached Rome he refused to enter the city, but he appeared before the senate without the walls, in a very humble garb and with the most subdued and unassuming demeanor. He was no longer, he said, a Roman officer, or even citizen, but a Carthaginian prisoner, and he disavowed all right to direct, or even to counsel, the Roman authorities in respect to the proper course to be pursued. His opinion was, however, he said, that the Romans ought not to make peace or to exchange prisoners. He himself and the other Roman prisoners were old and infirm, and not worth the exchange; and, moreover, they had no claim whatever on their country, as they could only have been made prisoners in consequence of want of courage or patriotism to die in their country's cause. He said that the Carthaginians were tired of the war, and that their resources were exhausted, and that the Romans ought to press forward in it with renewed vigor, and leave himself and the other prisoners to their fate.

The senate came very slowly and reluctantly to the conclusion to follow this advice. They, however, all earnestly joined in attempting to persuade Regulus that he was under no obligation to return to Carthage. His promise, they said, was extorted by the circumstances of the case, and was not binding. Regulus, however, insisted on keeping his faith with his enemies. He sternly refused to see his family, and, bidding the senate farewell, he returned to Carthage. The Carthaginians, exasperated at his having himself interposed to prevent the success of his mission, tortured him for some time in the most cruel manner, and finally put him to death. One would think that he ought to have counseled peace and an exchange of prisoners, and he ought not to have refused to see his unhappy wife and children; but it was certainly very noble in him to refuse to break his word.

The war continued for some time after this, until, at length, both nations became weary of the contest, and peace was made. The following is the treaty which was signed. It shows that the advantage, on the whole, in this first Punic war, was on the part of the Romans:

"There shall be peace between Rome and Carthage. The Carthaginians shall evacuate all Sicily. They shall not make war upon any allies of the Romans. They shall restore to the Romans, without ransom, all the prisoners which they have taken from them, and pay them within ten years three thousand two hundred talents of silver."

The war had continued twenty-four years.

2

Hannibal Saguntum

THE name of Hannibal's father was Hamilcar. He was one of the leading Carthaginian generals. He occupied a very prominent position, both on account of his rank, and wealth, and high family connections at Carthage, and also on account of the great military energy which he displayed in the command of the armies abroad. He carried on the wars which the Carthaginians waged in Africa and in Spain after the conclusion of the war with the Romans, and he longed to commence hostilities with the Romans again.

At one time, when Hannibal was about nine years of age, Hamilcar was preparing to set off on an expedition into Spain, and, as was usual in those days, he was celebrating the occasion with games, and spectacles, and various religious ceremonies. It has been the custom in all ages of the world, when nations go to war with each other, for each side to take measures for propitiating the favor of Heaven. Christian nations at the present day do it by prayers offered in each country for the success of their own arms. Heathen nations do it by sacrifices, libations, and offerings. Hamilcar had made arrangements for such sacrifices, and the priests were offering them in the presence of the whole assembled army.

Young Hannibal, then about nine years of age, was present. He was a boy of great spirit and energy, and he entered with much enthusiasm into the scene. He wanted to go to Spain himself with the army, and he came to his father and began to urge his request. His father could not consent to this. He was too young to endure the privations and fatigues of such an enterprise. However, his father brought him to one of the altars, in the presence of the other officers of the army, and made him lay his hand upon the consecrated victim, and swear that, as soon as he was old enough, and had it in his power, he would make war upon the Romans. This was done, no doubt, in part to amuse young Hannibal's mind, and to relieve his disappointment in not being able to go to war at that time, by promising him a great and mighty enemy to fight at some future day. Hannibal remembered it, and longed for the time to come when he could go to war against the Romans.

Hamilcar bade his son farewell and embarked for Spain. He was at liberty to extend his conquests there in all directions west of the River Iberus, a river which the reader will find upon the map, flowing southeast into the Mediterranean Sea. Its name, Iberus, has been gradually changed, in modern times, to Ebro. By the treaty with the Romans the Carthaginians were not to cross the Iberus. They were also bound by the treaty not to molest the people of Saguntum, a city lying between the Iberus and the Carthaginian dominions. Saguntum was in alliance with the Romans and under their protection.

Hamilcar was, however, very restless and uneasy at being obliged thus to refrain from hostilities with the Roman power. He began, immediately after his arrival in Spain, to form plans for renewing the war. He had under him, as his principal lieutenant, a young man who had married his daughter. His name was Hasdrubal. With Hasdrubal's aid he went on extending his conquests in Spain, and strengthening his position there, and gradually maturing his plans for renewing war with the Romans, when at length he died. Hasdrubal succeeded him. Hannibal was now, probably, about twenty-one or two years old, and still in Carthage. Hasdrubal sent to the Carthaginian government a request that Hannibal might receive an appointment in the army, and be sent out to join him in Spain.

On the subject of complying with this request there was a great debate in the Carthaginian senate. In all cases where questions of government are controlled by votes, it has been found, in every age, that parties will always be formed, of which the two most prominent will usually be nearly balanced one against the other. Thus, at this time, though the Hamilcar family were in power, there was a very strong party in Carthage in opposition to them. The leader of this party in the senate, whose name was Hanno, made a very earnest speech against sending Hannibal. He was too young, he said, to be of any service. He would only learn the vices and follies of the camp, and thus become corrupted and ruined. "Besides," said Hanno, "at this rate, the command of our armies in Spain is getting to be a sort of hereditary right. Hamilcar was not a king, that his authority should thus descend first to his son-in-law and then to his son; for this plan of making Hannibal," he said, "while yet scarcely arrived at manhood, a high officer in the army, is only a stepping-stone to the putting of the forces wholly under his orders, whenever, for any reason, Hasdrubal shall cease to command them."

The Roman historian, through whose narrative we get our only account of this debate, says that, though these were good reasons, yet strength prevailed, as usual, over wisdom, in the decision of the question. They voted to send Hannibal, and he set out to cross the sea to Spain with a heart full of enthusiasm and joy.

A great deal of curiosity and interest was felt throughout the army to see him on his arrival. The soldiers had been devotedly attached to his father, and they were all ready to transfer this attachment at once to the son, if he should prove worthy of it. It was very evident, soon after he reached the camp, that he was going to prove himself thus worthy. He entered at once into the duties of his position with a degree of energy, patience, and self-denial which attracted universal attention, and made him a universal favorite. He dressed plainly; he assumed no airs; he sought for no pleasures or indulgences, nor demanded any exemption from the dangers and privations which the common soldiers had to endure. He ate plain food, and slept, often in his military cloak, on the ground, in the midst of the soldiers on guard; and in battle he was always foremost to press forward into the contest, and the last to leave the ground when the time came for repose. The Romans say that, in addition to these qualities, he was inhuman and merciless when in open warfare with his foes, and cunning and treacherous in every other mode of dealing with them. It is very probable that he was so. Such traits of character were considered by soldiers in those days, as they are now, virtues in themselves, though vices in their enemies.

However this may be, Hannibal became a great and universal favorite in the army. He went on for several years increasing his military knowledge, and widening and extending his influence, when at length, one day, Hasdrubal was suddenly killed by a ferocious native of the country whom he had by some means offended. As soon as the first shock of this occurrence was over, the leaders of the army went in pursuit of Hannibal, whom they brought in triumph to the tent of Hasdrubal, and instated him at once in the supreme command, with one consent and in the midst of universal acclamations. As soon as news of this event reached Carthage, the government there confirmed the act of the army, and Hannibal thus found himself suddenly but securely invested with a very high military command.

His eager and restless desire to try his strength with the Romans received a new impulse by his finding that the power was now in his hands. Still the two countries were at peace. They were bound by solemn treaties to continue so. The River Iberus was the boundary which separated the dominions of the two nations from each other in Spain, the territory east of that boundary being under the Roman power, and that on the west under that of the Carthaginians; except that Saguntum, which was on the western side, was an ally of the Romans, and the Carthaginians were bound by the treaty to leave it independent and free.

Hannibal could not, therefore, cross the Iberus or attack Saguntum without an open infraction of the treaty. He, however, immediately began to move toward Saguntum, and to attack the nations in the immediate vicinity of it. If he wished to get into a war with the Romans, this was the proper way to promote it; for, by advancing thus into the immediate vicinity of the capital of their allies, there was great probability that disputes would arise which would sooner or later end in war.

The Romans say that Hannibal was cunning and treacherous, and he certainly did display, on some occasions, a great degree of adroitness in his stratagems. In one instance in these preliminary wars he gained a victory over an immensely superior force in a very remarkable manner. He was returning from an inroad upon some of the northern provinces, laden and encumbered with spoil, when he learned that an immense army, consisting, it was said, of a hundred thousand men, were coming down upon his rear. There was a river at a short distance before him. Hannibal pressed on and crossed the river by a ford, the water being, perhaps, about three feet deep. He secreted a large body of cavalry near the bank of the stream, and pushed on with the main body of the army to some little distance from the river, so as to produce the impression upon his pursuers that he was pressing forward to make his escape.

The Battle in the River.

The enemy, thinking that they had no time to lose, poured down in great numbers into the stream from various points along the banks; and, as soon as they had reached the middle of the current, and were wading laboriously, half submerged, with their weapons held above their heads, so as to present as little resistance as possible to the water, the horsemen of Hannibal rushed in to meet and attack them. The horsemen had, of course, greatly the advantage; for, though their horses were in the water, they were themselves raised above it, and their limbs were free, while their enemies were half submerged, and, being encumbered by their arms and by one another, were nearly helpless. They were immediately thrown into complete confusion, and were overwhelmed and carried down by the current in great numbers. Some of them succeeded in landing below, on Hannibal's side; but, in the mean time, the main body of his army had returned, and was ready to receive them, and they were trampled under foot by the elephants, which it was the custom to employ, in those days, as a military force. As soon as the river was cleared, Hannibal marched his own army across it, and attacked what remained of the enemy on their own side. He gained a complete victory, which was so great and decisive that he secured by it possession of the whole country west of the Iberus, except Saguntum, and Saguntum itself began to be seriously alarmed.

The Saguntines sent embassadors to Rome to ask the Romans to interpose and protect them from the dangers which threatened them. These embassadors made diligent efforts to reach Rome as soon as possible, but they were too late. On some pretext or other, Hannibal contrived to raise a dispute between the city and one of the neighboring tribes, and then, taking sides with the tribe, he advanced to attack the city. The Saguntines prepared for their defense, hoping soon to receive succors from Rome. They strengthened and fortified their walls, while Hannibal began to move forward great military engines for battering them down.

Hannibal knew very well that by his hostilities against this city he was commencing a contest with Rome itself, as Rome must necessarily take part with her ally. In fact, there is no doubt that his design was to bring on a general war between the two great nations. He began with Saguntum for two reasons: first, it would not be safe for him to cross the Iberus, and advance into the Roman territory, leaving so wealthy and powerful a city in his rear; and then, in the second place, it was easier for him to find pretexts for getting indirectly into a quarrel with Saguntum, and throwing the odium of a declaration of war on Rome, than to persuade the Carthaginian state to renounce the peace and themselves commence hostilities. There was, as has been already stated, a very strong party at Carthage opposed to Hannibal, who would, of course, resist any measures tending to a war with Rome, for they would consider such a war as opening a vast field for gratifying Hannibal's ambition. The only way, therefore, was to provoke a war by aggressions on the Roman allies, to be justified by the best pretexts he could find.

Saguntum was a very wealthy and powerful city. It was situated about a mile from the sea. The attack upon the place, and the defense of it by the inhabitants, went on for some time with great vigor. In these operations, Hannibal exposed himself to great danger. He approached, at one time, so near the wall, in superintending the arrangements of his soldiers and the planting of his engines, that a heavy javelin, thrown from the parapet, struck him on the thigh. It pierced the flesh, and inflicted so severe a wound that he fell immediately, and was borne away by the soldiers. It was several days before he was free from the danger incurred by the loss of blood and the fever which follows such a wound. During all this time his army were in a great state of excitement and anxiety, and suspended their active operations. As soon, however, as Hannibal was found to be decidedly convalescent, they resumed them again, and urged them onward with greater energy than before.

The weapons of warfare in those ancient days were entirely different from those which are now employed, and there was one, described by an ancient historian as used by the Saguntines at this siege, which might almost come under the modern denomination of fire-arms. It was called the falarica. It was a sort of javelin, consisting of a shaft of wood, with a long point of iron. This point was said to be three feet long. This javelin was to be thrown at the enemy either from the hand of the soldier or by an engine. The leading peculiarity of it was, however, that, near to the pointed end, there were wound around the wooden shaft long bands of tow, which were saturated with pitch and other combustibles, and this inflammable band was set on fire just before the javelin was thrown. As the missile flew on its way, the wind fanned the flames, and made them burn so fiercely, that when the javelin struck the shield of the soldier opposing it, it could not be pulled out, and the shield itself had to be thrown down and abandoned.

While the inhabitants of Saguntum were vainly endeavoring to defend themselves against their terrible enemy by these and similar means, their embassadors, not knowing that the city had been attacked, had reached Rome, and had laid before the Roman senate their fears that the city would be attacked, unless they adopted vigorous and immediate measures to prevent it. The Romans resolved to send embassadors to Hannibal to demand of him what his intentions were, and to warn him against any acts of hostility against Saguntum. When these Roman embassadors arrived on the coast, near to Saguntum, they found that hostilities had commenced, and that the city was hotly besieged. They were at a loss to know what to do.

It is better for a rebel not to hear an order which he is determined beforehand not to obey. Hannibal, with an adroitness which the Carthaginians called sagacity, and the Romans treachery and cunning, determined not to see these messengers. He sent word to them, at the shore, that they must not attempt to come to his camp, for the country was in such a disturbed condition that it would not be safe for them to land; and besides, he could not receive or attend to them, for he was too much pressed with the urgency of his military works to have any time to spare for debates and negotiations.

Hannibal knew that the embassadors, being thus repulsed, and having found, too, that the war had broken out, and that Saguntum was actually beset and besieged by Hannibal's armies, would proceed immediately to Carthage to demand satisfaction there. He knew, also, that Hanno and his party would very probably espouse the cause of the Romans, and endeavor to arrest his designs. He accordingly sent his own embassadors to Carthage, to exert an influence in his favor in the

Carthaginian senate, and endeavor to urge them to reject the claims of the Romans, and allow the war between Rome and Carthage to break out again.

The Roman embassadors appeared at Carthage, and were admitted to an audience before the senate. They stated their case, representing that Hannibal had made war upon Saguntum in violation of the treaty, and had refused even to receive the communication which had been sent him by the Roman senate through them. They demanded that the Carthaginian government should disavow his acts, and deliver him up to them, in order that he might receive the punishment which his violation of the treaty, and his aggressions upon an ally of the Romans, so justly deserved.

The party of Hannibal in the Carthaginian senate were, of course, earnest to have these proposals rejected with scorn. The other side, with Hanno at their head, maintained that they were reasonable demands. Hanno, in a very energetic and powerful speech, told the senate that he had warned them not to send Hannibal into Spain. He had foreseen that such a hot and turbulent spirit as his would involve them in inextricable difficulties with the Roman power. Hannibal had, he said, plainly violated the treaty. He had invested and besieged Saguntum, which they were solemnly bound not to molest, and they had nothing to expect in return but that the Roman legions would soon be investing and besieging their own city. In the mean time, the Romans, he added, had been moderate and forbearing. They had brought nothing to the charge of the Carthaginians. They accused nobody but Hannibal, who, thus far, alone was guilty. The Carthaginians, by disavowing his acts, could save themselves from the responsibility of them. He urged, therefore, that an embassage of apology should be sent to Rome, that Hannibal should be deposed and delivered up to the Romans, and that ample restitution should be made to the Saguntines for the injuries they had received.

On the other hand, the friends of Hannibal urged in the Carthaginian senate their defense of the general. They reviewed the history of the transactions in which the war had originated, and showed, or attempted to show, that the Saguntines themselves commenced hostilities, and that consequently they, and not Hannibal, were responsible for all that followed; that, under those circumstances, the Romans ought not to take their part, and if they did so, it proved that they preferred the friendship of Saguntum to that of Carthage; and that it would be cowardly and dishonorable in the extreme for them to deliver the general whom they had placed in power, and who had shown himself so worthy of their choice by his courage and energy, into the hands of their ancient and implacable foes.

Thus Hannibal was waging at the same time two wars, one in the Carthaginian senate, where the weapons were arguments and eloquence, and the other under the walls of Saguntum, which was fought with battering rams and fiery javelins. He conquered in both. The senate decided to send the Roman embassadors home without acceding to their demands, and the walls of Saguntum were battered down by Hannibal's engines. The inhabitants refused all terms of compromise, and resisted to the last, so that, when the victorious soldiery broke over the prostrate walls, and poured into the city, it was given up to them to plunder, and they killed and destroyed all that came in their way. The disappointed embassadors returned to Rome with the news that Saguntum had been taken and destroyed by Hannibal, and that the Carthaginians, far from offering any satisfaction for the wrong, assumed the responsibility of it themselves, and were preparing for war.

Thus Hannibal accomplished his purpose of opening the way for waging war against the Roman power. He prepared to enter into the contest with the utmost energy and zeal. The conflict that ensued lasted seventeen years, and is known in history as the second Punic war. It was one of the most dreadful struggles between rival and hostile nations which the gloomy history of mankind exhibits to view. The events that occurred will be described in the subsequent chapters.

3

Opening of the Second Punic War

WHEN the tide once turns in any nation in favor of war, it generally rushes on with great impetuosity and force, and bears all before it. It was so in Carthage in this instance. The party of Hanno were thrown entirely into the minority and silenced, and the friends and partisans of Hannibal carried not only the government, but the whole community with them, and every body was eager for war. This was owing, in part, to the natural contagiousness of the martial spirit, which, when felt by one, catches easily, by sympathy, in the heart of another. It is a fire which, when once it begins to burn, spreads in every direction, and consumes all that comes in its way.

Besides, when Hannibal gained possession of Saguntum, he found immense treasures there, which he employed, not to increase his own private fortune, but to strengthen and confirm his civil and military power. The Saguntines did every thing they could to prevent these treasures from falling into his hands. They fought desperately to the last, refused all terms of surrender, and they became so insanely desperate in the end, that, according to the narrative of Livy, when they found that the walls and towers of the city were falling in, and that all hope of further defense was gone, they built an enormous fire in the public streets, and heaped upon it all the treasures which they had time to collect that fire could destroy, and then that many of the principal inhabitants leaped into the flames themselves, in order that their hated conquerors might lose their prisoners as well as their spoils.

Notwithstanding this, however, Hannibal obtained a vast amount of gold and silver, both in the form of money and of plate, and also much valuable merchandise, which the Saguntine merchants had accumulated in their palaces and warehouses. He used all this property to strengthen his own political and military position. He paid his soldiers all the arrears due to them in full. He divided among them a large additional amount as their share of the spoil. He sent rich trophies home to Carthage, and presents, consisting of sums of money, and jewelry, and gems, to his friends here, and to those whom he wished to make his friends. The result of this munificence, and of the renown which his victories in Spain had procured for him, was to raise him to the highest pinnacle of influence and honor. The Carthaginians chose him one of the suffetes.

The suffetes were the supreme executive officers of the Carthaginian commonwealth. The government was, as has been remarked before, a sort of aristocratic republic, and republics are always very cautious about intrusting power, even executive power, to any one man. As Rome had two consuls, reigning jointly, and France, after her first revolution, a Directory of five, so the Carthaginians chose annually two suffetes, as they were called at Carthage, though the Roman writers call them indiscriminately suffetes, consuls, and kings; so that, in conjunction with his colleague, he held the supreme civil authority in Carthage, besides being invested with the command of the vast and victorious army in Spain.

When news of these events—the siege and destruction of Saguntum, the rejection of the demands of the Roman embassadors, and the vigorous preparations making by the Carthaginians for war—reached Rome, the whole city was thrown into consternation. The senate and the people held tumultuous and disorderly assemblies, in which the events which had occurred, and the course of proceeding which it was incumbent on the Romans to take, were discussed with much excitement and clamor. The Romans were, in fact, afraid of the Carthaginians. The campaigns of Hannibal in Spain had impressed the people with a strong sense of remorseless and terrible energy of his character; they at once concluded that his plans would be formed for marching into Italy, and they even anticipated the danger of his bringing the war up to the very gates of the city, so as to threaten them with the destruction which he had brought upon Saguntum. The event showed how justly they appreciated his character.

Since the conclusion of the first Punic war, there had been peace between the Romans and Carthaginians for about a quarter of a century. During all this time both nations had been advancing in wealth and power, but the Carthaginians had made much more rapid progress than the Romans. The Romans had, indeed, been very successful at the outset in the former war, but in the end the Carthaginians had proved themselves their equal. They seemed, therefore, to dread now a fresh encounter with these powerful foes, led on, as they were now to be, by such a commander as Hannibal.

They determined, therefore, to send a second embassy to Carthage, with a view of making one more effort to preserve peace before actually commencing hostilities. They accordingly selected five men from among the most influential citizens of the state—men of venerable age and of great public consideration—and commissioned them to proceed to Carthage and ask once more whether it was the deliberate and final decision of the Carthaginian senate to avow and sustain the action of Hannibal. This solemn embassage set sail. They arrived at Carthage. They appeared before the senate. They argued their cause, but it was, of course, to deaf and unwilling ears. The Carthaginian orators replied to them, each side attempting to throw the blame of the violation of the treaty on the other. It was a solemn hour, for the peace of the world, the lives of hundreds of thousands of men, and the continued happiness or the desolation and ruin of vast regions of country, depended on the issue of the debate.

Unhappily, the breach was only widened by the discussion. "Very well," said the Roman commissioners, at last, "we offer you peace or war, which do you choose?" "Whichever you please," replied the Carthaginians; "decide for yourselves." "War, then," said the Romans, "since it must be so." The conference was broken up, and the embassadors returned to Rome.

They returned, however, by the way of Spain. Their object in doing this was to negotiate with the various kingdoms and tribes in Spain and in France, through which Hannibal would have to march in invading Italy, and endeavor to induce them to take sides with the Romans. They were too late, however, for Hannibal had contrived to extend and establish his influence in all that region too strongly to be shaken; so that, on one pretext or another, the Roman proposals were all rejected. There was one powerful tribe, for example, called the Volscians. The embassadors, in the presence of the great council of the Volscians, made known to them the probability of war, and invited them to ally themselves with the Romans. The Volscians rejected the proposition with a sort of scorn. "We see," said they, "from the fate of Saguntum, what is to be expected to result from an alliance with the Romans. After leaving that city defenseless and alone in its struggle against such terrible danger, it is in vain to ask other nations to trust to your protection. If you wish for new allies, it will be best for you to go where the story of Saguntum is not known." This answer of the Volscians was applauded by the other nations of Spain, as far as it was known, and the Roman embassadors, despairing of success in that country, went on into Gaul, which is the name by which the country now called France is known in ancient history.

On reaching a certain place which was a central point of influence and power in Gaul, the Roman commissioners convened a great martial council there. The spectacle presented by this assembly was very imposing, for the warlike counselors came to the meeting armed completely and in the most formidable manner, as if they were coming to a battle instead of a consultation and debate. The venerable embassadors laid the subject before them. They descanted largely on the power and greatness of the Romans, and on the certainty that they should conquer in the approaching contest, and they invited the Gauls to espouse their cause, and to rise in arms and intercept Hannibal's passage through their country, if he should attempt to effect one.

The assembly could hardly be induced to hear the embassadors through; and, as soon as they had finished their address, the whole council broke forth into cries of dissent and displeasure, and even into shouts of derision. Order was at length restored, and the officers, whose duty it was to express the sentiments of the assembly, gave for their reply that the Gauls had never received any thing but violence and injuries from Rome, or any thing but kindness and good-will from Carthage; and that they had no idea of being guilty of the folly of bringing the impending storm of Hannibal's hostility upon their own heads, merely for the sake of averting it from their ancient and implacable foes. Thus the embassadors were every where repulsed. They found no friendly disposition toward the Roman power till they had crossed the Rhone.

Hannibal began now to form his plans, in a very deliberate and cautious manner, for a march into Italy. He knew well that this was an expedition of such magnitude and duration as to require beforehand the most careful and well-considered arrangements, both for the forces which were to go, and for the states and communities which were to remain. The winter was coming on. His first measure was to dismiss a large portion of his forces, that they might visit their homes. He told them that he was intending some great designs for the ensuing spring, which might take them to a great distance, and keep them for a long time absent from Spain, and he would, accordingly, give them the intervening time to visit their families and their homes, and to arrange their affairs. This act of kind consideration and confidence renewed the attachment of the soldiers to their commander, and they returned to his camp in the spring not only with new strength and vigor, but with redoubled attachment to the service in which they were engaged.

Hannibal, after sending home his soldiers, retired himself to New Carthage, which, as will be seen by the map, is further west than Saguntum, where he went into winter quarters, and devoted himself to the maturing of his designs. Besides the necessary preparations for his own march, he had to provide for the government of the countries that he should leave. He devised various and ingenious plans to prevent the danger of insurrections and rebellions while he was gone. One was, to organize an army for Spain out of soldiers drawn from Africa, while the troops which were to be employed to garrison Carthage, and to sustain the government there, were taken from Spain. By thus changing the troops of the two countries, each country was controlled by a foreign soldiery, who were more likely to be faithful in their obedience to their commanders, and less in danger of sympathizing with the populations which they were respectively employed to control, than if each had been retained in its own native land.

Hannibal knew very well that the various states and provinces of Spain, which had refused to ally themselves with the Romans and abandon him, had been led to do this through the influence of his presents or the fear of his power, and that if, after he had penetrated into Italy, he should meet with reverses, so as to diminish very much their hope of deriving benefit from his favor or their fear of his power, there would be great danger of defections and revolts. As an additional security against this, he adopted the following ingenious plan. He enlisted a body of troops from among all the nations of Spain that were in alliance with him, selecting the young men who were enlisted as much as possible from families of consideration and influence, and this body of troops, when organized and officered, he sent into Carthage, giving the nations and tribes from which they were drawn to understand that he considered them not only as soldiers serving in his armies, but as hostages, which he should hold as security for the fidelity and obedience of the countries from which they had come. The number of these soldiers was four thousand.

Hannibal had a brother, whose name, as it happened, was the same as that of his brother-in-law, Hasdrubal. It was to him that he committed the government of Spain during his absence. The soldiers provided for him were, as has been already stated, mainly drawn from Africa. In addition to the foot soldiers, he provided him with a small body of horse. He left with him, also, fourteen elephants. And as he thought it not improbable that the Romans might, in some contingency during his absence, make a descent upon the Spanish coast from the sea, he built and equipped for him a small fleet of about sixty vessels, fifty of which were of the first class. In modern times, the magnitude and efficiency of a ship is estimated by the number of guns she will carry; then, it was the number of banks of oars. Fifty of Hasdrubal's ships were quinqueremes, as they were called, that is, they had five banks of oars.

The Romans, on the other hand, did not neglect their own preparations. Though reluctant to enter upon the war, they still prepared to engage in it with their characteristic energy and ardor, when they found that it could not be averted. They resolved on raising two powerful armies, one for each of the consuls. The plan was, with one of these to advance to meet Hannibal, and with the other to proceed to Sicily, and from Sicily to the African coast, with a view of threatening the Carthaginian capital. This plan, if successful, would compel the Carthaginians to recall a part or the whole of Hannibal's army from the intended invasion of Italy to defend their own African homes.

The force raised by the Romans amounted to about seventy thousand men. About a third of these were Roman soldiers, and the remainder were drawn from various nations dwelling in Italy and in the islands of the Mediterranean Sea which were in alliance with the Romans. Of these troops six thousand were cavalry. Of course, as the Romans intended to cross into Africa, they needed a fleet. They built and equipped one, which consisted of two hundred and twenty ships of the largest class, that is, quinqueremes, besides a number of smaller and lighter vessels for services requiring speed. There were vessels in use in those times larger than the quinqueremes. Mention is occasionally made of those which had six and even seven banks of oars. But these were only employed as the flag-ships of commanders, and for other purposes of ceremony and parade, as they were too unwieldy for efficient service in action.

Lots were then drawn in a very solemn manner, according to the Roman custom on such occasions, to decide on the assignment of these two armies to the respective consuls. The one destined to meet Hannibal on his way from Spain, fell to a consul named Cornelius Scipio. The name of the other was Sempronius. It devolved on him, consequently, to take charge of the expedition destined to Sicily and Africa. When all the arrangements were thus made, the question was finally put, in a very solemn and formal manner, to the Roman people for their final vote and decision. "Do the Roman people decide and decree that war shall be declared against the Carthaginians?" The decision was in the affirmative. The war was then proclaimed with the usual imposing ceremonies. Sacrifices and religious celebrations followed, to propitiate the favor of the gods, and to inspire the soldiers with that kind of courage and confidence which the superstitious, however wicked, feel when they can imagine themselves under the protection of heaven. These shows and spectacles being over, all things were ready.

In the mean time Hannibal was moving on, as the spring advanced, toward the banks of the Iberus, that frontier stream, the crossing of which made him an invader of what was, in some sense, Roman territory. He boldly passed the stream, and moved forward along the coast of the Mediterranean, gradually approaching the Pyrenees, which form the boundary between France and Spain. His soldiers hitherto did not know what his plans were. It is very little the custom now for military and naval commanders to communicate to their men much information about their designs, and it was still less the custom then; and besides, in those days, the common soldiers had no access to those means of information by which news of every sort is now so universally diffused. Thus, though all the officers of the army, and well-informed citizens both in Rome and Carthage, anticipated and understood Hannibal's designs, his own soldiers, ignorant and degraded, knew nothing except that they were to go on some distant and dangerous service. They, very likely, had no idea whatever of Italy or of Rome, or of the magnitude of the possessions, or of the power held by the vast empire which they were going to invade.

When, however, after traveling day after day, they came to the foot of the Pyrenees, and found that they were really going to pass that mighty chain of mountains, and for this purpose were actually entering its wild and gloomy defiles, the courage of some of them failed, and they began to murmur. The discontent and alarm were, in fact, so great, that one corps, consisting of about three thousand men, left the camp in a body, and moved back toward their homes. On inquiry, Hannibal found that there were ten thousand more who were in a similar state of feeling. His whole force consisted of over one hundred thousand. And now what does the reader imagine that Hannibal would do in such an emergency? Would he return in pursuit of these deserters, to recapture and destroy them as a terror to the rest? Or would he let them go, and attempt by words of conciliation and encouragement to confirm and save those that yet remained? He did neither. He called together the ten thousand discontented troops that were still in his camp, and told them that, since they were afraid to accompany his army, or unwilling to do so, they might return. He wanted none in his service who had not the courage and fortitude to go on wherever he might lead. He would not have the faint-hearted and the timid in his army. They would only be a burden to load down and impede the courage and energy of the rest. So saying, he gave orders for them to return, and with the rest of the army, whose resolution and ardor were redoubled by this occurrence, he moved on through the passes of the mountains.

This act of Hannibal, in permitting his discontented soldiers to return, had all the effect of a deed of generosity in its influence upon the minds of the soldiers who went on. We must not, however, imagine that it was prompted by a spirit of generosity at all. It was policy. A seeming generosity was, in this case, exactly what was wanted to answer his ends.

Hannibal was mercilessly cruel in all cases where he imagined that severity was demanded. It requires great sagacity sometimes in a commander to know when he must punish, and when it is wisest to overlook and forgive. Hannibal, like Alexander and Napoleon, possessed this sagacity in a very high degree; and it was, doubtless, the exercise of that principle alone which prompted his action on this occasion.

Thus Hannibal passed the Pyrenees. The next difficulty that he anticipated was in crossing the River Rhone.

4

The Passage of the Rhone

HANNIBAL, after he had passed the Pyrenees, did not anticipate any new difficulty till he should arrive at the Rhone. He knew very well that that was a broad and rapid river, and that he must cross it near its mouth, where the water was deep and the banks low; and, besides, it was not impossible that the Romans who were coming to meet him, under Cornelius Scipio, might have reached the Rhone before he should arrive there, and be ready upon the banks to dispute his passage. He had sent forward, therefore, a small detachment in advance, to reconnoiter the country and select a route to the Rhone, and if they met with no difficulties to arrest them there, they were to go on till they reached the Alps, and explore the passages and defiles through which his army could best cross those snow-covered mountains.

It seems that before he reached the Pyrenees—that is, while he was upon the Spanish side of them, some of the tribes through whose territories he had to pass undertook to resist him, and he, consequently, had to attack them and reduce them by force; and then, when he was ready to move on, he left a guard in the territories thus conquered to keep them in subjection. Rumors of this reached Gaul. The Gauls were alarmed for their own safety. They had not intended to oppose Hannibal so long as they supposed that he only wished for a safe passage through their country on his way to Italy; but now, when they found, from what had occurred in Spain, that he was going to conquer the countries he traversed as he passed along, they became alarmed. They seized their arms, and assembled in haste at Ruscino, and began to devise measures of defense. Ruscino was the same place as that in which the Roman embassadors met the great council of the Gauls on their return to Italy from Carthage.

While this great council, or, rather, assembly of armies, was gathering at Ruscino, full of threats and anger, Hannibal was at Illiberis, a town at the foot of the Pyrenean Mountains. He seems to have had no fear that any opposition which the Gauls could bring to bear against him would be successful, but he dreaded the delay. He was extremely unwilling to spend the precious months of the early summer in contending with such foes as they, when the road to Italy was before him. Besides, the passes of the Alps, which are difficult and laborious at any time, are utterly impracticable except in the months of July and August. At all other seasons they are, or were in those days, blocked up with impassable snows. In modern times roads have been made, with galleries cut through the rock, and with the exposed places protected by sloping roofs projecting from above, over which storms sweep and avalanches slide without injury; so that now the intercourse of ordinary travel between France and Italy, across the Alps, is kept up, in some measure, all the year. In Hannibal's time, however, the mountains could not be traversed except in the summer months, and if it had not been that the result justified the undertaking, it would have been considered an act of inexcusable rashness and folly to attempt to cross with an army at all.

Hannibal had therefore no time to lose, and that circumstance made this case one of those in which forbearance and a show of generosity were called for, instead of defiance and force. He accordingly sent messengers to the council at Ruscino to say, in a very complaisant and affable manner, that he wished to see and confer with their princes in person, and that, if they pleased, he would advance for this purpose toward Ruscino; or they might, if they preferred, come on toward him at Illiberis, where he would await their arrival. He invited them to come freely into his camp, and said that he was ready, if they were willing to receive him, to go into theirs, for he had come to Gaul as a friend and an ally, and wanted nothing but a free passage through their territory. He had made a resolution, he said, if the Gauls would but allow him to keep it, that there should not be a single sword drawn in his army till he got into Italy.

The alarm and the feelings of hostility which prevailed among the Gauls were greatly allayed by this message. They put their camp in motion, and went on to Illiberis. The princes and high officers of their armies went to Hannibal's camp, and were received with the highest marks of distinction and honor. They were loaded with presents, and went away charmed with the affability, the wealth, and the generosity of their visitor. Instead of opposing his progress, they became the conductors and guides of his army. They took them first to Ruscino, which was, as it were, their capital, and thence, after a short delay, the army moved on without any further molestation toward the Rhone.

In the mean time, the Roman consul Scipio, having embarked the troops destined to meet Hannibal in sixty ships at the mouth of the Tiber, set sail for the mouth of the Rhone. The men were crowded together in the ships, as armies necessarily must be when transported by sea. They could not go far out to sea, for, as they had no compass in those days, there were no means of directing the course of navigation, in case of storms or cloudy skies, except by the land. The ships accordingly made their way slowly along the shore, sometimes by means of sails and sometimes by oars, and, after suffering for some time the hardships and privations incident to such a voyage—the sea-sickness and the confinement of such swarming numbers in so narrow a space bringing every species of discomfort in their train—the fleet entered the mouth of the Rhone. The officers had no idea that Hannibal was near. They had only heard of his having crossed the Iberus. They imagined that he was still on the other side of the Pyrenees. They entered the Rhone by the first branch they came to—for the Rhone, like the Nile, divides near its mouth, and flows into the sea by several separate channels—and sailed without concern up to Marseilles, imagining that their enemy was still hundreds of miles away, entangled, perhaps, among the defiles of the Pyrenees. Instead of that, he was safely encamped upon the banks of the Rhone, a short distance above them, quietly and coolly making his arrangements for crossing it.

When Cornelius got his men upon the land, they were too much exhausted by the sickness and misery they had endured upon the voyage to move on to meet Hannibal without some days for rest and refreshment. Cornelius, however, selected three hundred horsemen who were able to move, and sent them up the river on an exploring expedition, to learn the facts in respect to Hannibal, and to report them to him. Dispatching them accordingly, he remained himself in his camp, reorganizing and recruiting his army, and awaiting the return of the party that he had sent to explore.

Although Hannibal had thus far met with no serious opposition in his progress through Gaul, it must not, on that account, be supposed that the people, through whose territories he was passing, were really friendly to his cause, or pleased with his presence among them. An army is always a burden and a curse to any country that it enters, even when its only object is to pass peacefully through. The Gauls assumed a friendly attitude toward this dreaded invader and his horde only because they thought that by so doing he would the sooner pass and be gone. They were too weak, and had too few means of resistance to attempt to stop him; and, as the next best thing that they could do, resolved to render him every possible aid to hasten him on. This continued to be the policy of the various tribes until he reached the river. The people on the further side of the river, however, thought it was best for them to resist. They were nearer to the Roman territories, and, consequently, somewhat more under Roman influence. They feared the resentment of the Romans if they should, even passively, render any co-operation to Hannibal in his designs; and, as they had the broad and rapid river between them and their enemy, they thought there was a reasonable prospect that, with its aid, they could exclude him from their territories altogether.

Thus it happened that, when Hannibal came to the stream, the people on one side were all eager to promote, while those on the other were determined to prevent his passage, both parties being animated by the same desire to free their country from such a pest as the presence of an army of ninety thousand men; so that Hannibal stood at last upon the banks of the river, with the people on his side of the stream waiting and ready to furnish all the boats and vessels that they could command, and to render every aid in their power in the embarkation, while those on the other were drawn up in battle array, rank behind rank, glittering with weapons, marshaled so as to guard every place of landing, and lining with pikes the whole extent of the shore, while the peaks of their tents, in vast numbers, with banners among them floating in the air, were to be seen in the distance behind them. All this time, the three hundred horsemen which Cornelius had dispatched, were slowly and cautiously making their way up the river from the Roman encampment below.

After contemplating the scene presented to his view at the river for some time in silence, Hannibal commenced his preparations for crossing the stream. He collected first all the boats of every kind which could be obtained among the Gauls who lived along the bank of the river. These, however, only served for a beginning, and so he next got together all the workmen and all the tools which the country could furnish, for several miles around, and went to work constructing more. The Gauls of that region had a custom of making boats of the trunks of large trees. The tree, being felled and cut to the proper length, was hollowed out with hatchets and adzes, and then, being turned bottom upward, the outside was shaped in such a manner as to make it glide easily through the water. So convenient is this mode of making boats, that it is practiced, in cases where sufficiently large trees are found, to the present day. Such boats are now called canoes.

There were plenty of large trees on the banks of the Rhone. Hannibal's soldiers watched the Gauls at their work, in making boats of them, until they learned the art themselves. Some first assisted their new allies in the easier portions of the operation, and then began to fell large trees and make the boats themselves. Others, who had less skill or more impetuosity chose not to wait for the slow process of hollowing the wood, and they, accordingly, would fell the trees upon the shore, cut the trunks of equal lengths, place them side by side in the water, and bolt or bind them together so as to form a raft. The form and fashion of their craft was of no consequence, they said, as it was for one passage only. Any thing would answer, if it would only float and bear its burden over.

In the mean time, the enemy upon the opposite shore looked on, but they could do nothing to impede these operations. If they had had artillery, such as is in use at the present day, they could have fired across the river, and have blown the boats and rafts to pieces with balls and shells as fast as the Gauls and Carthaginians could build them. In fact, the workmen could not have built them under such a cannonading; but the enemy, in this case, had nothing but spears, and arrows, and stones, to be thrown either by the hand, or by engines far too weak to send them with any effect across such a stream. They had to look on quietly, therefore, and allow these great and formidable preparations for an attack upon them to go on without interruption. Their only hope was to overwhelm the army with their missiles, and prevent their landing, when they should reach the bank at last in their attempt to cross the stream.

If an army is crossing a river without any enemy to oppose them, a moderate number of boats will serve, as a part of the army can be transported at a time, and the whole gradually transferred from one bank to the other by repeated trips of the same conveyances. But when there is an enemy to encounter at the landing, it is necessary to provide the means of carrying over a very large force at a time; for if a small division were to go over first alone, it would only throw itself, weak and defenseless, into the hands of the enemy. Hannibal, therefore, waited until he had boats, rafts, and floats enough constructed to carry over a force all together sufficiently numerous and powerful to attack the enemy with a prospect of success.

The Romans, as we have already remarked, say that Hannibal was cunning. He certainly was not disposed, like Alexander, to trust in his battles to simple superiority of bravery and force, but was always contriving some stratagem to increase the chances of victory. He did so in this case. He kept up for many days a prodigious parade and bustle of building boats and rafts in sight of his enemy, as if his sole reliance was on the multitude of men that he could pour across the river at a single transportation, and he thus kept their attention closely riveted upon these preparations. All this time, however, he had another plan in course of execution. He had sent a strong body of troops secretly up the river, with orders to make their way stealthily through the forests, and cross the stream some few miles above. This force was intended to move back from the river, as soon as it should cross the stream, and come down upon the enemy in the rear, so as to attack and harass them there at the same time that Hannibal was crossing with the main body of the army. If they succeeded in crossing the river safely, they were to build a fire in the woods, on the other side, in order that the column of smoke which should ascend from it might serve as a signal of their success to Hannibal.

This detachment was commanded by an officer named Hanno—of course a very different man from Hannibal's great enemy of that name in Carthage. Hanno set out in the night, moving back from the river, in commencing his march, so as to be entirely out of sight from the Gauls on the other side. He had some guides, belonging to the country, who promised to show him a convenient place for crossing. The party went up the river about twenty-five miles. Here they found a place where the water spread to a greater width, and where the current was less rapid, and the water not so deep. They got to this place in silence and secrecy, their enemies below not having suspected any such design. As they had, therefore, nobody to oppose them, they could cross much more easily than the main army below. They made some rafts for carrying over those of the men that could not swim, and such munitions of war as would be injured by the wet. The rest of the men waded till they reached the channel, and then swam, supporting themselves in part by their bucklers, which they placed beneath their bodies in the water. Thus they all crossed in safety. They paused a day, to dry their clothes and to rest, and then moved cautiously down the river until they were near enough to Hannibal's position to allow their signal to be seen. The fire was then built, and they gazed with exultation upon the column of smoke which ascended from it high into the air.

Hannibal saw the signal, and now immediately prepared to cross with his army. The horsemen embarked in boats, holding their horses by lines, with a view of leading them into the water so that they might swim in company with the boats. Other horses, bridled and accoutered, were put into large flat-bottomed boats, to be taken across dry, in order that they might be all ready for service at the instant of landing. The most vigorous and efficient portion of the army were, of course, selected for the first passage, while all those who, for any cause, were weak or disabled, remained behind, with the stores and munitions of war, to be transported afterward, when the first passage should have been effected. All this time the enemy, on the opposite shore, were getting their ranks in array, and making every thing ready for a furious assault upon the invaders the moment they should approach the land.

There was something like silence and order during the period while the men were embarking and pushing out from the land, but as they advanced into the current, the loud commands, and shouts, and outcries increased more and more, and the rapidity of the current and of the eddies by which the boats and rafts were hurried down the stream, or whirled against each other, soon produced a terrific scene of tumult and confusion. As soon as the first boats approached the land, the Gauls assembled to oppose them rushed down upon them with showers of missiles, and with those unearthly yells which barbarous warriors always raise in going into battle, as a means both of exciting themselves and of terrifying their enemy. Hannibal's officers urged the boats on, and endeavored, with as much coolness and deliberation as possible, to effect a landing. It is perhaps doubtful how the contest would have ended, had it not been for the detachment under Hanno, which now came suddenly into action. While the Gauls were in the height of their excitement, in attempting to drive back the Carthaginians from the bank, they were thunderstruck at hearing the shouts and cries of an enemy behind them, and, on looking around, they saw the troops of Hanno pouring down upon them from the thickets with terrible impetuosity and force. It is very difficult for an army to fight both in front and in the rear at the same time. The Gauls, after a brief struggle, abandoned the attempt any longer to oppose Hannibal's landing. They fled down the river and back into the interior, leaving Hanno in secure possession of the bank, while Hannibal and his forces came up at their leisure out of the water, finding friends instead of enemies to receive them.

The remainder of the army, together with the stores and munitions of war, were next to be transported, and this was accomplished with little difficulty now that there was no enemy to disturb their operations. There was one part of the force, however, which occasioned some trouble and delay. It was a body of elephants which formed a part of the army. How to get these unwieldy animals across so broad and rapid a river was a question of no little difficulty. There are various accounts of the manner in which Hannibal accomplished the object, from which it would seem that different methods were employed. One mode was as follows: the keeper of the elephants selected one more spirited and passionate in disposition than the rest, and contrived to teaze and torment him so as to make him angry. The elephant advanced toward his keeper with his trunk raised to take vengeance. The keeper fled; the elephant pursued him, the other elephants of the herd following, as is the habit of the animal on such occasions. The keeper ran into the water as if to elude his pursuer, while the elephant and a large part of the herd pressed on after him. The man swam into the channel, and the elephants, before they could check themselves, found that they were beyond their depth. Some swam on after the keeper, and crossed the river, where they were easily secured. Others, terrified, abandoned themselves to the current, and were floated down, struggling helplessly as they went, until at last they grounded upon shallows or points of land, whence they gained the shore again, some on one side of the stream and some on the other.

This plan was thus only partially successful, and Hannibal devised a more effectual method for the remainder of the troop. He built an immensely large raft, floated it up to the shore, fastened it there securely, and covered it with earth, turf, and bushes, so as to make it resemble a projection of the land. He then caused a second raft to be constructed of the same size, and this he brought up to the outer edge of the other, fastened it there by a temporary connection, and covered and concealed it as he had done the first. The first of these rafts extended two hundred feet from the shore, and was fifty feet broad. The other, that is, the outer one, was only a little smaller. The soldiers then contrived to allure and drive the elephants over these rafts to the outer one, the animals imagining that they had not left the land. The two rafts were then disconnected from each other, and the outer one began to move with its bulky passengers over the water, towed by a number of boats which had previously been attached to its outer edge.

The Elephants Crossing the Rhone.

As soon as the elephants perceived the motion, they were alarmed, and began immediately to look anxiously this way and that, and to crowd toward the edges of the raft which was conveying them away. They found themselves hemmed in by water on every side, and were terrified and thrown into confusion. Some were crowded off into the river, and were drifted down till they landed below. The rest soon became calm, and allowed themselves to be quietly ferried across the stream, when they found that all hope of escape and resistance were equally vain.

In the mean time, while these events were occurring, the troop of three hundred, which Scipio had sent up the river to see what tidings he could learn of the Carthaginians, were slowly making their way toward the point where Hannibal was crossing; and it happened that Hannibal had sent down a troop of five hundred, when he first reached the river, to see if they could learn any tidings of the Romans. Neither of the armies had any idea how near they were to the other. The two detachments met suddenly and unexpectedly on the way. They were sent to explore, and not to fight; but as they were nearly equally matched, each was ambitious of the glory of capturing the others and carrying them prisoners to their camp. They fought a long and bloody battle. A great number were killed, and in about the same proportion on either side. The Romans say they conquered. We do not know what the Carthaginians said, but as both parties retreated from the field and went back to their respective camps, it is safe to infer that neither could boast of a very decisive victory.

5

Hannibal Crosses the Alps

IT is difficult for any one who has not actually seen such mountain scenery as is presented by the Alps, to form any clear conception of its magnificence and grandeur. Hannibal had never seen the Alps, but the world was filled then, as now, with their fame.

Some of the leading features of sublimity and grandeur which these mountains exhibit, result mainly from the perpetual cold which reigns upon their summits. This is owing simply to their elevation. In every part of the earth, as we ascend from the surface of the ground into the atmosphere, it becomes, for some mysterious reason or other, more and more cold as we rise, so that over our heads, wherever we are, there reigns, at a distance of two or three miles above us, an intense and perpetual cold. This is true not only in cool and temperate latitudes, but also in the most torrid regions of the globe. If we were to ascend in a balloon at Borneo at midday, when the burning sun of the tropics was directly over our heads, to an elevation of five or six miles, we should find that although we had been moving nearer to the sun all the time, its rays would have lost, gradually, all their power. They would fall upon us as brightly as ever, but their heat would be gone. They would feel like moonbeams, and we should be surrounded with an atmosphere as frosty as that of the icebergs of the frigid zone.

It is from this region of perpetual cold that hail-stones descend upon us in the midst of summer, and snow is continually forming and falling there; but the light and fleecy flakes melt before they reach the earth, so that, while the hail has such solidity and momentum that it forces its way through, the snow dissolves, and falls upon us as a cool and refreshing rain. Rain cools the air around us and the ground, because it comes from cooler regions of the air above.

Now it happens that not only the summits, but extensive portions of the upper declivities of the Alps, rise into the region of perpetual winter. Of course, ice congeals continually there, and the snow which forms falls to the ground as snow, and accumulates in vast and permanent stores. The summit of Mount Blanc is covered with a bed of snow of enormous thickness, which is almost as much a permanent geological stratum of the mountain as the granite which lies beneath it.

Of course, during the winter months, the whole country of the Alps, valley as well as hill, is covered with snow. In the spring the snow melts in the valleys and plains, and higher up it becomes damp and heavy with partial melting, and slides down the declivities in vast avalanches, which sometimes are of such enormous magnitude, and descend with such resistless force, as to bring down earth, rocks, and even the trees of the forest in their train. On the higher declivities, however, and over all the rounded summits, the snow still clings to its place, yielding but very little to the feeble beams of the sun, even in July.

There are vast ravines and valleys among the higher Alps where the snow accumulates, being driven into them by winds and storms in the winter, and sliding into them, in great avalanches, in the spring. These vast depositories of snow become changed into ice below the surface; for at the surface there is a continual melting, and the water, flowing down through the mass, freezes below. Thus there are valleys, or rather ravines, some of them two or three miles wide and ten or fifteen miles long, filled with ice, transparent, solid, and blue, hundreds of feet in depth. They are called glaciers. And what is most astonishing in respect to these icy accumulations is that, though the ice is perfectly compact and solid, the whole mass is found to be continually in a state of slow motion down the valley in which it lies, at the rate of about a foot in twenty-four hours. By standing upon the surface and listening attentively, we hear, from time to time, a grinding sound. The rocks which lie along the sides are pulverized, and are continually moving against each other and falling; and then, besides, which is a more direct and positive proof still of the motion of the mass, a mark may be set up upon the ice, as has been often done, and marks corresponding to it made upon the solid rocks on each side of the valley, and by this means the fact of the motion, and the exact rate of it, may be fully ascertained.

Thus these valleys are really and literally rivers of ice, rising among the summits of the mountains, and flowing, slowly it is true, but with a continuous and certain current, to a sort of mouth in some great and open valley below. Here the streams which have flowed over the surface above, and descended into the mass through countless crevices and chasms; into which the traveler looks down with terror, concentrate and issue from under the ice in a turbid torrent, which comes out from a vast archway made by the falling in of masses which the water has undermined. This lower end of the glacier sometimes presents a perpendicular wall hundreds of feet in height; sometimes it crowds down into the fertile valley, advancing in some unusually cold summer into the cultivated country, where, as it slowly moves on, it plows up the ground, carries away the orchards and fields, and even drives the inhabitants from the villages which it threatens. If the next summer proves warm, the terrible monster slowly draws back its frigid head, and the inhabitants return to the ground it reluctantly evacuates, and attempt to repair the damage it has done.

The Alps lie between France and Italy, and the great valleys and the ranges of mountain land lie in such a direction that they must be crossed in order to pass from one country to the other. These ranges are, however, not regular. They are traversed by innumerable chasms, fissures, and ravines; in some places they rise in vast rounded summits and swells, covered with fields of spotless snow; in others they tower in lofty, needle-like peaks, which even the chamois can not scale, and where scarcely a flake of snow can find a place of rest. Around and among these peaks and summits, and through these frightful defiles and chasms, the roads twist and turn, in a zigzag and constantly ascending course, creeping along the most frightful precipices, sometimes beneath them and sometimes on the brink, penetrating the darkest and gloomiest defiles, skirting the most impetuous and foaming torrents, and at last, perhaps, emerging upon the surface of a glacier, to be lost in interminable fields of ice and snow, where countless brooks run in glassy channels, and crevasses yawn, ready to take advantage of any slip which may enable them to take down the traveler into their bottomless abysses.

And yet, notwithstanding the awful desolation which reigns in the upper regions of the Alps, the lower valleys, through which the streams finally meander out into the open plains, and by which the traveler gains access to the sublimer scenes of the upper mountains, are inexpressibly verdant and beautiful. They are fertilized by the deposits of continual inundations in the early spring, and the sun beats down into them with a genial warmth in summer, which brings out millions of flowers, of the most beautiful forms and colors, and ripens rapidly the broadest and richest fields of grain. Cottages, of every picturesque and beautiful form, tenanted by the cultivators, the shepherds and the herdsmen, crown every little swell in the bottom of the valley, and cling to the declivities of the mountains which rise on either hand. Above them eternal forests of firs and pines wave, feathering over the steepest and most rocky slopes with their somber foliage. Still higher, gray precipices rise, and spires and pinnacles, far grander and more picturesque, if not so symmetrically formed, than those constructed by man. Between these there is seen, here and there, in the background, vast towering masses of white and dazzling snow, which crown the summits of the loftier mountains beyond.

Hannibal's determination to carry an army into Italy by way of the Alps, instead of transporting them by galleys over the sea, has always been regarded as one of the greatest undertakings of ancient times. He hesitated for some time whether he should go down the Rhone, and meet and give battle to Scipio, or whether he should leave the Roman army to its course, and proceed himself directly toward the Alps and Italy. The officers and soldiers, of the army, who had now learned something of their destination and of their leader's plans, wanted to go and meet the Romans. They dreaded the Alps. They were willing to encounter a military foe, however formidable, for this was a danger that they were accustomed to and could understand; but their imaginations were appalled at the novel and awful images they formed of falling down precipices of ragged rocks, or of gradually freezing, and being buried half alive, during the process, in eternal snows.

Hannibal, when he found that his soldiers were afraid to proceed, called the leading portions of his army together, and made them an address. He remonstrated with them for yielding now to unworthy fears, after having successfully met and triumphed over such dangers as they had already incurred. "You have surmounted the Pyrenees," said he, "you have crossed the Rhone. You are now actually in sight of the Alps, which are the very gates of access to the country of the enemy. What do you conceive the Alps to be? They are nothing but high mountains, after all. Suppose they are higher than the Pyrenees, they do not reach to the skies; and, since they do not, they can not be insurmountable. They are surmounted, in fact, every day; they are even inhabited and cultivated, and travelers continually pass over them to and fro. And what a single man can do, an army can do, for an army is only a large number of single men. In fact, to a soldier, who has nothing to carry with him but the implements of war, no way can be too difficult to be surmounted by courage and energy."

After finishing his speech, Hannibal, finding his men reanimated and encouraged by what he had said, ordered them to go to their tents and refresh themselves, and prepare to march on the following day. They made no further opposition to going on. Hannibal did not, however, proceed at once directly toward the Alps. He did not know what the plans of Scipio might be, who, it will be recollected, was below him, on the Rhone, with the Roman army. He did not wish to waste his time and his strength in a contest with Scipio in Gaul, but to press on and get across the Alps into Italy as soon as possible. And so, fearing lest Scipio should strike across the country, and intercept him if he should attempt to go by the most direct route, he determined to move northwardly, up the River Rhone, till he should get well into the interior, with a view of reaching the Alps ultimately by a more circuitous journey.

It was, in fact, the plan of Scipio to come up with Hannibal and attack him as soon as possible; and, accordingly, as soon as his horsemen or, rather, those who were left alive after the battle had returned and informed him that Hannibal and his army were near, he put his camp in motion and moved rapidly up the river. He arrived at the place where the Carthaginians had crossed a few days after they had gone. The spot was in a terrible state of ruin and confusion. The grass and herbage were trampled down for the circuit of a mile, and all over the space were spots of black and smouldering remains, where the camp-fires had been kindled. The tops and branches of trees lay every where around, their leaves withering in the sun, and the groves and forests were encumbered with limbs, and rejected trunks, and trees felled and left where they lay. The shore was lined far down the stream with ruins of boats and rafts, with weapons which had been lost or abandoned, and with the bodies of those who had been drowned in the passage, or killed in the contest on the shore. These and numerous other vestiges remained but the army was gone.

There were, however, upon the ground groups of natives and other visitors, who had come to look at the spot now destined to become so memorable in history. From these men Scipio learned when and where Hannibal had gone. He decided that it was useless to attempt to pursue him. He was greatly perplexed to know what to do. In the casting of lots, Spain had fallen to him, but now that the great enemy whom he had come forth to meet had left Spain altogether, his only hope of intercepting his progress was to sail back into Italy, and meet him as he came down from the Alps into the great valley of the Po. Still, as Spain had been assigned to him as his province, he could not well entirely abandon it. He accordingly sent forward the largest part of his army into Spain, to attack the forces that Hannibal had left there, while he himself, with a smaller force, went down to the sea-shore and sailed back to Italy again. He expected to find Roman forces in the valley of the Po, with which he hoped to be strong enough to meet Hannibal as he descended from the mountains, if he should succeed in effecting a passage over them.

In the mean time Hannibal went on, drawing nearer and nearer to the ranges of snowy summits which his soldiers had seen for many days in their eastern horizon. These ranges were very resplendent and grand when the sun went down in the west, for then it shone directly upon them. As the army approached nearer and nearer to them, they gradually withdrew from sight and disappeared, being concealed by intervening summits less lofty, but nearer. As the soldiers went on, however, and began to penetrate the valleys, and draw near to the awful chasms and precipices among the mountains, and saw the turbid torrents descending from them, their fears revived. It was, however, now too late to retreat. They pressed forward; ascending continually, till their road grew extremely precipitous and insecure, threading its way through almost impassable defiles, with rugged cliffs overhanging them, and snowy summits towering all around.

At last they came to a narrow defile through which they must necessarily pass, but which was guarded by large bodies of armed men assembled on the rocks and precipices above, ready to hurl stones and weapons of every kind upon them if they should attempt to pass through. The army halted. Hannibal ordered then to encamp where they were, until he could consider what to do. In the course of the day he learned that the mountaineers did not remain at their elevated posts during the night, on account of the intense cold and exposure, knowing, too, that it would be impossible for an army to traverse such a pass as they were attempting to guard without daylight to guide them, for the road, or rather pathway, which passes through these defiles, follows generally the course of a mountain torrent, which flows through a succession of frightful ravines and chasms, and often passes along on a shelf or projection of the rock, hundreds and sometimes thousands of feet from the bed of the stream, which foams and roars far below. There could, of course, be no hope of passing safely by such a route without the light of day.

The mountaineers, therefore, knowing that it was not necessary to guard the pass at night—its own terrible danger being then a sufficient protection—were accustomed to disperse in the evening, and descend to regions where they could find shelter and repose, and to return and renew their watch in the morning. When Hannibal learned this, he determined to anticipate them in getting up upon the rocks the next day, and, in order to prevent their entertaining any suspicion of his design, he pretended to be making all the arrangements for encamping for the night on the ground he had taken. He accordingly pitched more tents, and built, toward evening, a great many fires, and he began some preparations indicating that it was his intention the next day to force his way through the pass. He moved forward a strong detachment up to a point near the entrance to the pass, and put them in a fortified position there, as if to have them all ready to advance when the proper time should arrive on the following day.

The mountaineers, seeing all these preparations going on, looked forward to a conflict on the morrow, and, during the night, left their positions as usual, to descend to places of shelter. The next morning, however, when they began, at an early hour, to ascend to them again, they were astonished to find all the lofty rocks, and cliffs, and shelving projections which overhung the pass, covered with Carthaginians. Hannibal had aroused a strong body of his men at the earliest dawn, and led them up, by steep climbing, to the places which the mountaineers had left, so as to be there before them. The mountaineers paused, astonished, at this spectacle, and their disappointment and rage were much increased on looking down into the valley below, and seeing there the remainder of the Carthaginian army quietly moving through the pass in a long train, safe apparently from any molestation, since friends, and not enemies, were now in possession of the cliffs above.

The mountaineers could not restrain their feelings of vexation and anger, but immediately rushed down the declivities which they had in part ascended, and attacked the army in the defile. An awful scene of struggle and confusion ensued. Some were killed by weapons or by rocks rolled down upon them. Others, contending together, and struggling desperately in places of very narrow foothold, tumbled headlong down the rugged rocks into the torrent below; and horses, laden with baggage and stores, became frightened and unmanageable, and crowded each other over the most frightful precipices. Hannibal, who was above on the higher rocks, looked down upon this scene for a time with the greatest anxiety and terror. He did not dare to descend himself and mingle in the affray, for fear of increasing the confusion. He soon found, however, that it was absolutely necessary for him to interpose, and he came down as rapidly as possible, his detachment with him. They descended by oblique and zigzag paths, wherever they could get footing among the rocks, and attacked the mountaineers with great fury. The result was, as he had feared, a great increase at first of the confusion and the slaughter. The horses were more and more terrified by the fresh energy of the combat, and by the resounding of louder shouts and cries, which were made doubly terrific by the echoes and reverberations of the mountains. They crowded against each other, and fell, horses and men together, in masses, over the cliffs to the rugged rocks below, where they lay in confusion, some dead, and others dying, writhing helplessly in agony, or vainly endeavoring to crawl away.

The mountaineers were, however, conquered and driven away at last, and the pass was left clear. The Carthaginian column was restored to order. The horses that had not fallen were calmed and quieted. The baggage which had been thrown down was gathered up, and the wounded men were placed on litters, rudely constructed on the spot, that they might be borne on to a place of safety. In a short time all were ready to move on, and the march was accordingly recommenced. There was no further difficulty. The column advanced in a quiet and orderly manner until they had passed the defile. At the extremity of it they came to a spacious fort belonging to the natives. Hannibal took possession of this fort, and paused for a little time there to rest and refresh his men.

One of the greatest difficulties encountered by a general in conducting an army through difficult and dangerous roads, is that of providing food for them. An army can transport its own food only a very little way. Men traveling over smooth roads can only carry provisions for a few days, and where the roads are as difficult and dangerous as the passes of the Alps, they can scarcely carry any. The commander must, accordingly, find subsistence in the country through which he is marching. Hannibal had, therefore, now not only to look out for the safety of his men, but their food was exhausted, and he must take immediate measures to secure a supply.

The lower slopes of lofty mountains afford usually abundant sustenance for flocks and herds. The showers which are continually falling there, and the moisture which comes down the sides of the mountains through the ground, keep the turf perpetually green, and sheep and cattle love to pasture upon it; they climb to great heights, finding the herbage finer and sweeter the higher they go. Thus the inhabitants of mountain ranges are almost always shepherds and herdsmen. Grain can be raised in the valleys below, but the slopes of the mountains, though they produce grass to perfection, are too steep to be tilled.

As soon as Hannibal had got established in the fort, he sent around small bodies of men to seize and drive in all the cattle and sheep that they could find. These men were, of course, armed, in order that they might be prepared to meet any resistance which they might encounter. The mountaineers, however, did not attempt to resist them. They felt that they were conquered, and they were accordingly disheartened and discouraged. The only mode of saving their cattle which was left to them, was to drive them as fast as they could into concealed and inaccessible places. They attempted to do this, and while Hannibal's parties were ranging up the valleys all around them, examining every field, and barn, and sheepfold that they could find, the wretched and despairing inhabitants were flying in all directions, driving the cows and sheep, on which their whole hope of subsistence depended, into the fastnesses of the mountains. They urged them into wild thickets, and dark ravines and chasms, and over dangerous glaciers, and up the steepest ascents, wherever there was the readiest prospect of getting them out of the plunderer's way.

These attempts, however, to save their little property were but very partially successful. Hannibal's marauding parties kept coming home, one after another, with droves of sheep and cattle before them, some larger and some smaller, but making up a vast amount in all. Hannibal subsisted his men three days on the food thus procured for them. It requires an enormous store to feed ninety or a hundred thousand men, even for three days; besides, in all such cases as this, an army always waste and destroy far more than they really consume.

During these three days the army was not stationary, but was moving slowly on. The way, though still difficult and dangerous, was at least open before them, as there was now no enemy to dispute their passage. So they went on, rioting upon the abundant supplies they had obtained, and rejoicing in the double victory they were gaining, over the hostility of the people and the physical dangers and difficulties of the way. The poor mountaineers returned to their cabins ruined and desolate, for mountaineers who have lost their cows and their sheep have lost their all.

The Alps are not all in Switzerland. Some of the most celebrated peaks and ranges are in a neighboring state called Savoy. The whole country is, in fact, divided into small states, called cantons at the present day, and similar political divisions seem to have existed in the time of the Romans. In his march onward from the pass which has been already described, Hannibal, accordingly, soon approached the confines of another canton. As he was advancing slowly into it, with the long train of his army winding up with him through the valleys, he was met at the borders of this new state by an embassage sent from the government of it. They brought with them fresh stores of provisions, and a number of guides. They said that they had heard of the terrible destruction which had come upon the other canton in consequence of their effort to oppose his progress, and that they had no intention of renewing so vain an attempt. They came, therefore, they said, to offer Hannibal their friendship and their aid. They had brought guides to show the army the best way over the mountains, and a present of provisions; and to prove the sincerity of their professions they offered Hannibal hostages. These hostages were young men and boys, the sons of the principal inhabitants, whom they offered to deliver into Hannibal's power, to be kept by him until he should see that they were faithful and true in doing what they offered.

Hannibal on the Alps.

Hannibal was so accustomed to stratagem and treachery himself, that he was at first very much at a loss to decide whether these offers and professions were honest and sincere, or whether they were only made to put him off his guard. He thought it possible that it was their design to induce him to place himself under their direction, so that they might lead him into some dangerous defile or labyrinth of rocks, from which he could not extricate himself, and where they could attack and destroy him. He, however, decided to return them a favorable answer, but to watch them very carefully, and to proceed under their guidance with the utmost caution and care. He accepted of the provisions they offered, and took the hostages. These last he delivered into the custody of a body of his soldiers, and they marched on with the rest of the army. Then, directing the new guides to lead the way, the army moved on after them. The elephants went first, with a moderate force for their protection preceding and accompanying them. Then came long trains of horses and mules, loaded with military stores and baggage, and finally the foot soldiers followed, marching irregularly in a long column. The whole train must have extended many miles, and must have appeared from any of the eminences around like an enormous serpent, winding its way tortuously through the wild and desolate valleys.

Hannibal was right in his suspicions. The embassage was a stratagem. The men who sent it had laid an ambuscade in a very narrow pass, concealing their forces in thickets and in chasms, and in nooks and corners among the rugged rocks, and when the guides had led the army well into the danger, a sudden signal was given, and these concealed enemies rushed down upon them in great numbers, breaking into their ranks, and renewing the scene of terrible uproar, tumult, and destruction which had been witnessed in the other defile. One would have thought that the elephants, being so unwieldy and so helpless in such a scene, would have been the first objects of attack. But it was not so. The mountaineers were afraid of them. They had never seen such animals before, and they felt for them a mysterious awe, not knowing what terrible powers such enormous beasts might be expected to wield. They kept away from them, therefore, and from the horsemen, and poured down upon the head of the column of foot soldiers which followed in the rear.

They were quite successful at the first onset. They broke through the head of the column, and drove the rest back. The horses and elephants, in the mean time, moved forward, bearing the baggage with them, so that the two portions of the army were soon entirely separated. Hannibal was behind, with the soldiers. The mountaineers made good their position, and, as night came on, the contest ceased, for in such wilds as these no one can move at all, except with the light of day. The mountaineers, however, remained in their place, dividing the army, and Hannibal continued, during the night, in a state of great suspense and anxiety, with the elephants and the baggage separated from him, and apparently at the mercy of the enemy.

During the night he made vigorous preparations for attacking the mountaineers the next day. As soon as the morning light appeared, he made the attack, and he succeeded in driving the enemy away, so far, at least, as to allow him to get his army together again. He then began once more to move on. The mountaineers, however, hovered about his way, and did all they could to molest and embarrass his march. They concealed themselves in ambuscades, and attacked the Carthaginians as they passed. They rolled stones down upon them, or discharged spears and arrows from eminences above; and if any of Hannibal's army became, from any reason, detached from the rest, they would cut off their retreat, and then take them prisoners or destroy them. Thus they gave Hannibal a great deal of trouble. They harassed his march continually, without presenting at any point a force which he could meet and encounter in battle. Of course, Hannibal could no longer trust to his guides, and he was obliged to make his way as he best could, sometimes right, but often wrong, and exposed to a thousand difficulties and dangers, which those acquainted with the country might have easily avoided. All this time the mountaineers were continually attacking him, in bands like those of robbers, sometimes in the van, and sometimes in the rear, wherever the nature of the ground or the circumstances of the marching army afforded them an opportunity.

Hannibal persevered, however, through all these discouragements, protecting his men as far as it was in his power, but pressing earnestly on, until in nine days he reached the summit. By the summit, however, is not meant the summit of the mountains, but the summit of the pass, that is, the highest point which it was necessary for him to attain in going over. In all mountain ranges there are depressions, which are in

Switzerland called necks, and the pathways and roads over the ranges lie always in these. In America, such a depression in a ridge of land, if well marked and decided, is called a notch. Hannibal attained the highest point of the col, by which he was to pass over, in nine days after the great battle. There were, however, of course, lofty peaks and summits towering still far above him.

He encamped here two days to rest and refresh his men. The enemy no longer molested him. In fact, parties were continually coming into the camp, of men and horses, that had got lost, or had been left in the valleys below. They came in slowly, some wounded, others exhausted and spent by fatigue and exposure. In some cases horses came in alone. They were horses that had slipped or stumbled, and fallen among the rocks, or had sunk down exhausted by their toil, and had thus been left behind, and afterward, recovering their strength, had followed on, led by a strange instinct to keep to the tracks which their companions had made, and thus they rejoined the camp at last in safety.

In fact, one great reason for Hannibal's delay at his encampment on or near the summit of the pass, was to afford time for all the missing men to join the army again, that had the power to do so. Had it not been for this necessity, he would doubtless have descended some distance, at least, to a more warm and sheltered position before seeking repose. A more gloomy and desolate resting-place than the summit of an Alpine pass can scarcely be found. The bare and barren rocks are entirely destitute of vegetation, and they have lost, besides, the sublime and picturesque forms which they assume further below. They spread in vast, naked fields in every direction around the spectator, rising in gentle ascents, bleak and dreary, the surface whitened as if bleached by the perpetual rains. Storms are, in fact, almost perpetual in these elevated regions. The vast cloud which, to the eye of the shepherd in the valley below, seems only a fleecy cap, resting serenely upon the summit, or slowly floating along the sides, is really a driving mist, or cold and stormy rain, howling dismally over interminable fields of broken rocks, as if angry that it can make nothing grow upon them, with all its watering. Thus there are seldom distant views to be obtained, and every thing near presents a scene of simple dreariness and desolation.

Hannibal's soldiers thus found themselves in the midst of a dismal scene in their lofty encampment. There is one special source of danger, too, in such places as this, which the lower portions of the mountains are less exposed to, and that is the entire obliteration of the pathway by falls of snow. It seems almost absurd to speak of pathway in such regions, where there is no turf to be worn, and the boundless fields of rocks, ragged and hard, will take no trace of footsteps. There are, however, generally some faint traces of way, and where these fail entirely the track is sometimes indicated by small piles of stones, placed at intervals along the line of route. An unpracticed eye would scarcely distinguish these little landmarks, in many cases, from accidental heaps of stones which lie every where around. They, however, render a very essential service to the guides and to the mountaineers, who have been accustomed to conduct their steps by similar aids in other portions of the mountains.

But when snow begins to fall, all these and every other possible means of distinguishing the way are soon entirely obliterated. The whole surface of the ground, or, rather, of the rocks, is covered, and all landmarks disappear. The little monuments become nothing but slight inequalities in the surface of the snow, undistinguishable from a thousand others. The air is thick and murky, and shuts off alike all distant prospects, and the shape and conformation of the land that is near; the bewildered traveler has not even the stars to guide him, as there is nothing but dark, falling flakes, descending from an impenetrable canopy of stormy clouds, to be seen in the sky.

Hannibal encountered a snow storm while on the summit of the pass, and his army were very much terrified by it. It was now November. The army had met with so many detentions and delays that their journey had been protracted to a late period. It would be unsafe to attempt to wait till this snow should melt again. As soon, therefore, as the storm ended, and the clouds cleared away, so as to allow the men to see the general features of the country around, the camp was broken up and the army put in motion. The soldiers marched through the snow with great anxiety and fear. Men went before to explore the way, and to guide the rest by flags and banners which they bore. Those who went first made paths, of course, for those who followed behind, as the snow was trampled down by their footsteps. Notwithstanding these aids, however, the army moved on very laboriously and with much fear.

At length, however, after descending a short distance, Hannibal, perceiving that they must soon come in sight of the Italian valleys and plains which lay beyond the Alps, went forward among the pioneers, who had charge of the banners by which the movements of the army were directed, and, as soon as the open country began to come into view, he selected a spot where the widest prospect was presented, and halted his army there to let them take a view of the beautiful country which now lay before them. The Alps are very precipitous on the Italian side. The descent is very sudden, from the cold and icy summits, to a broad expanse of the most luxuriant and sunny plains. Upon these plains, which were spread out in a most enchanting, landscape at their feet, Hannibal and his soldiers now looked down with exultation and delight. Beautiful lakes, studded with still more beautiful islands, reflected the beams of the sun. An endless succession of fields, in sober autumnal colors, with the cottages of the laborers and stacks of grain scattered here and there upon them, and rivers meandering through verdant meadows, gave variety and enchantment to the view.

Hannibal made an address to his officers and men, congratulating them on having arrived, at last, so near to a successful termination of their toils. "The difficulties of the way," he said, "are at last surmounted, and these mighty barriers that we have scaled are the walls, not only of Italy, but of Rome itself. Since we have passed the Alps, the Romans will have no protection against us remaining. It is only one battle, when we get down upon the plains, or at most two, and the great city itself will be entirely at our disposal."

The whole army were much animated and encouraged, both by the prospect which presented itself to their view, and by the words of Hannibal. They prepared for the descent, anticipating little difficulty; but they found, on recommencing their march, that their troubles were by no means over. The mountains are far steeper on the Italian side than on the other, and it was extremely difficult to find paths by which the elephants and the horses, and even the men, could safely descend. They moved on for some time with great labor and fatigue, until, at length, Hannibal, looking on before, found that the head of the column had stopped, and the whole train behind was soon jammed together, the ranks halting along the way in succession, as they found their path blocked up by the halting of those before them.

Hannibal sent forward to ascertain the cause of the difficulty, and found that the van of the army had reached a precipice down which it was impossible to descend. It was necessary to make a circuit in hopes of finding some practicable way of getting down. The guides and pioneers went on, leading the army after them, and soon got upon a glacier which lay in their way. There was fresh snow upon the surface, covering the ice and concealing the crevasses, as they are termed—that is, the great cracks and fissures which extend in the glaciers down through the body of the ice. The army moved on, trampling down the new snow, and making at first a good road-way by their footsteps; but very soon the old ice and snow began to be trampled up by the hoofs of the horses and the heavy tread of such vast multitudes of armed men. It softened to a great depth, and made the work of toiling through it an enormous labor. Besides, the surface of the ice and snow sloped steeply, and the men and beasts were continually falling or sliding down, and getting swallowed up in avalanches which their own weight set in motion, or in concealed crevasses where they sank to rise no more.

They, however, made some progress, though slowly, and with great danger. They at last got below the region of the snow, but here they encountered new difficulties in the abruptness and ruggedness of the rocks, and in the zigzag and tortuous direction of the way. At last they came to a spot where their further progress appeared to be entirely cut off by a large mass of rock, which it seemed necessary to remove in order to widen the passage sufficiently to allow them to go on. The Roman historian says that Hannibal removed these rocks by building great fires upon them, and then pouring on vinegar, which opened seams and fissures in them, by means of which the rocks could be split and pried to pieces with wedges and crowbars. On reading this account, the mind naturally pauses to consider the probability of its being true. As they had no gunpowder in those days, they were compelled to resort to some such method as the one above described for removing rocks. There are some species of rock which are easily cracked and broken by the action of fire. Others resist it. There seems, however, to be no reason obvious why vinegar should materially assist in the operation. Besides, we can not suppose that Hannibal could have had, at such a time and place, any very large supply of vinegar on hand. On the whole, it is probable that, if any such operation was performed at all, it was on a very small scale, and the results must have been very insignificant at the time, though the fact has since been greatly celebrated in history.

In coming over the snow, and in descending the rocks immediately below, the army, and especially the animals connected with it, suffered a great deal from hunger. It was difficult to procure forage for them of any kind. At length however, as they continued their descent, they came first into the region of forests, and soon after to slopes of grassy fields descending into warm and fertile valleys. Here the animals were allowed to stop and rest, and renew their strength by abundance of food. The men rejoiced that their toils and dangers were over, and, descending easily the remainder of the way, they encamped at last safely on the plains of Italy.

6

Hannibal in the North of Italy

WHEN Hannibal's army found themselves on the plains of Italy, and sat down quietly to repose, they felt the effects of their fatigues and exposures far more sensibly than they had done under the excitement which they naturally felt while actually upon the mountains. They were, in fact, in a miserable condition. Hannibal told a Roman officer whom he afterward took prisoner that more than thirty thousand perished on the way in crossing the mountains; some in the battles which were fought in the passes, and a greater number still, probably, from exposure to fatigue and cold, and from falls among the rocks and glaciers, and diseases produced by destitution and misery. The remnant of the army which was left on reaching the plain were emaciated, sickly, ragged, and spiritless; far more inclined to lie down and die, than to go on and undertake the conquest of Italy and Rome.

After some days, however, they began to recruit. Although they had been half starved among the mountains, they had now plenty of wholesome food. They repaired their tattered garments and their broken weapons. They talked with one another about the terrific scenes through which they had been passing, and the dangers which they had surmounted, and thus, gradually strengthening their impressions of the greatness of the exploits they had performed, they began soon to awaken in each other's breasts an ambition to go on and undertake the accomplishment of other deeds of daring and glory.

We left Scipio with his army at the mouth of the Rhone, about to set sail for Italy with a part of his force, while the rest of it was sent on toward Spain. Scipio sailed along the coast by Genoa, and thence to Pisa, where he landed. He stopped a little while to recruit his soldiers after the voyage, and in the mean time sent orders to all the Roman forces then in the north of Italy to join his standard. He hoped in this way to collect a force strong enough to encounter Hannibal. These arrangements being made, he marched to the northward as rapidly as possible. He knew in what condition Hannibal's army had descended from the Alps, and wished to attack them before they should have time to recover from the effects of their privations and sufferings. He reached the Po before he saw any thing of Hannibal.

Hannibal, in the mean time, was not idle. As soon as his men were in a condition to move, he began to act upon the tribes that he found at the foot of the mountains, offering his friendship to some, and attacking others. He thus conquered those who attempted to resist him, moving, all the time, gradually southward toward the Po. That river has numerous branches, and among them is one named the Ticinus. It was on the banks of this river that the two armies at last came together.

Both generals must have felt some degree of solicitude in respect to the result of the contest which was about to take place. Scipio knew very well Hannibal's terrible efficiency as a warrior, and he was himself a general of great distinction, and a Roman, so that Hannibal had no reason to anticipate a very easy victory. Whatever doubts or fears, however, general officers may feel on the eve of an engagement, it is always considered very necessary to conceal them entirely from the men, and to animate and encourage the troops with a most undoubting confidence that they will gain the victory.

Both Hannibal and Scipio, accordingly, made addresses to their respective armies—at least so say the historians of those times—each one expressing to his followers the certainty that the other side would easily be beaten. The speech attributed to Scipio was somewhat as follows:

"I wish to say a few words to you, soldiers, before we go into battle. It is, perhaps, scarcely necessary. It certainly would not be necessary if I had now under my command the same troops that I took with me to the mouth of the Rhone. They knew the Carthaginians there, and would not have feared them here. A body of our horsemen met and attacked a larger body of theirs, and defeated them. We then advanced with our whole force toward their encampment, in order to give them battle. They, however, abandoned the ground and retreated before we reached the spot, acknowledging, by their flight, their own fear and our superiority. If you had been with us there, and had witnessed these facts, there would have been no need that I should say any thing to convince you now how easily you are going to defeat this Carthaginian foe.

"We have had a war with this same nation before. We conquered them then, both by land and sea; and when, finally, peace was made, we required them to pay us tribute, and we continued to exact it from them for twenty years. They are a conquered nation; and now this miserable army has forced its way insanely over the Alps, just to throw itself into our hands. They meet us reduced in numbers, and exhausted in resources and strength. More than half of their army perished in the mountains, and those that survive are weak, dispirited, ragged, and diseased. And yet they are compelled to meet us. If there was any chance for retreat, or any possible way for them to avoid the necessity of a battle, they would avail themselves of it. But there is not. They are hemmed in by the mountains, which are now, to them, an impassable wall, for they have not strength to scale them again. They are not real enemies; they are the mere remnants and shadows of enemies. They are wholly disheartened and discouraged, their strength and energy, both of soul and body, being spent and gone, through the cold, the hunger, and the squalid misery they have endured. Their joints are benumbed, their sinews stiffened, and their forms emaciated. Their armor is shattered and broken, their horses are lamed, and all their equipments worn out and ruined, so that really what most I fear is that the world will refuse us the glory of the victory, and say that it was the Alps that conquered Hannibal, and not the Roman army.

"Easy as the victory is to be, however, we must remember that there is a great deal at stake in the contest. It is not merely for glory that we are now about to contend. If Hannibal conquers, he will march to Rome, and our wives, our children, and all that we hold dear will be at his mercy. Remember this, and go into the battle feeling that the fate of Rome itself is depending upon the result."

An oration is attributed to Hannibal, too, on the occasion of this battle. He showed, however, his characteristic ingenuity and spirit of contrivance in the way in which he managed to attract strong attention to what he was going to say, by the manner in which he introduced it. He formed his army into a circle, as if to witness a spectacle. He then brought in to the center of this circle a number of prisoners that he had taken among the Alps—perhaps they were the hostages which had been delivered to him, as related in the preceding chapter. Whoever they were, however, whether hostages or captives taken in the battles which had been fought in the defiles, Hannibal had brought them with his army down into Italy, and now introducing them into the center of the circle which the army formed, he threw down before them such arms as they were accustomed to use in their native mountains, and asked them whether they would be willing to take those weapons and fight each other, on condition that each one who killed his antagonist should be restored to his liberty, and have a horse and armor given him, so that he could return home with honor. The barbarous monsters said readily that they would, and seized the arms with the greatest avidity. Two or three pairs of combatants were allowed to fight. One of each pair was killed, and the other set at liberty according to the promise of Hannibal. The combats excited the greatest interest, and awakened the strongest enthusiasm among the soldiers who witnessed them. When this effect had been sufficiently produced, the rest of the prisoners were sent away, and Hannibal addressed the vast ring of soldiery as follows:

"I have intended, soldiers, in what you have now seen, not merely to amuse you, but to give you a picture of your own situation. You are hemmed in on the right and left by two seas, and you have not so much as a single ship upon either of them. Then there is the Po before you and the Alps behind. The Po is a deeper, and more rapid and turbulent river than the Rhone; and as for the Alps, it was with the utmost difficulty that you passed over them when you were in full strength and vigor; they are an insurmountable wall to you now. You are therefore shut in, like our prisoners, on every side, and have no hope of life and liberty but in battle and victory.

"The victory, however, will not be difficult. I see, wherever I look among you, a spirit of determination and courage which I am sure will make you conquerors. The troops which you are going to contend against are mostly fresh recruits, that know nothing of the discipline of the camp, and can never successfully confront such war-worn veterans as you. You all know each other well, and me. I was, in fact, a pupil with you for many years, before I took the command. But Scipio's forces are strangers to one another and to him, and, consequently, have no common bond of sympathy; and as for Scipio himself, his very commission as a Roman general is only six months old.

"Think, too, what a splendid and prosperous career victory will open before you. It will conduct you to Rome. It will make you masters of one of the most powerful and wealthiest cities in the world. Thus far you have fought your battles only for glory or for dominion; now, you will have something more substantial to reward your success. There will be great treasures to be divided among you if we conquer, but if we are defeated we are lost. Hemmed in as we are on every side, there is no place that we can reach by flight. There is, therefore, no such alternative as flight left to us. We must conquer."

It is hardly probable that Hannibal could have really and honestly felt all the confidence that he expressed in his harangues to his soldiers. He must have had some fears. In fact, in all enterprises undertaken by man, the indications of success, and the hopes based upon them, will fluctuate from time to time, and cause his confidence in the result to ebb and flow, so that bright anticipations of success and triumph will alternate in his heart with feelings of discouragement and despondency. This effect is experienced by all; by the energetic and decided as well as by the timid and the faltering. The former, however, never allow these fluctuations of hope and fear to influence their action. They consider well the substantial grounds for expecting success before commencing their undertaking, and then go steadily forward, under all aspects of the sky—when it shines and when it rains—till they reach the end. The inefficient and undecided can act only under the stimulus of present hope. The end they aim at must be visibly before them all the time. If for a moment it passes out of view, their motive is gone, and they can do no more, till, by some change in circumstances, it comes in sight again.

Hannibal was energetic and decided. The time for him to consider whether he would encounter the hostility of the Roman empire, aroused to the highest possible degree, was when his army was drawn up upon the banks of the Iberus, before they crossed it. The Iberus was his Rubicon. That line once overstepped, there was to be no further faltering. The difficulties which arose from time to time to throw a cloud over his prospects, only seemed to stimulate him to fresh energy, and to awaken a new, though still a calm and steady resolution. It was so at the Pyrenees; it was so at the Rhone; it was so among the Alps, where the difficulties and daggers would have induced almost any other commander to have returned; and it was still so, now that he found himself shut in on every hand by the stern boundaries of Northern Italy, which he could not possibly hope again to pass, and the whole disposable force of the Roman empire, commanded, too, by one of the consuls, concentrated before him. The imminent danger produced no faltering, and apparently no fear.

The armies were not yet in sight of each other. They were, in fact, yet on opposite sides of the River Po. The Roman commander concluded to march his troops across the river, and advance in search of Hannibal, who was still at some miles' distance. After considering the various means of crossing the stream, he decided finally on building a bridge.

Military commanders generally throw some sort of a bridge across a stream of water lying in their way, if it is too deep to be easily forded, unless, indeed, it is so wide and rapid as to make the construction of the bridge difficult or impracticable. In this latter case they cross as well as they can by means of boats and rafts, and by swimming. The Po, though not a very large stream at this point, was too deep to be forded, and Scipio accordingly built a bridge. The soldiers cut down the trees which grew in the forests along the banks, and after trimming off the tops and branches, they rolled the trunks into the water. They placed these trunks side by side, with others, laid transversely and pinned down, upon the top. Thus they formed rafts, which they placed in a line across the stream, securing them well to each other and to the banks. This made the foundation for the bridge, and after this foundation was covered with other materials, so as to make the upper surface a convenient roadway, the army were conducted across it, and then a small detachment of soldiers were stationed at each extremity of it as a guard.

Such a bridge as this answers a very good temporary purpose, and in still water, as, for example, over narrow lakes or very sluggish streams, where there is very little current, a floating structure of this kind is sometimes built for permanent service. Such bridges will not, however, stand on broad and rapid rivers liable to floods. The pressure of the water alone, in such cases, would very much endanger all the fastenings; and in cases where drift wood or ice is brought down by the stream, the floating masses, not being able to pass under the bridge, would accumulate above it, and would soon bear upon it with so enormous a pressure that nothing could withstand its force. The bridge would be broken away, and the whole accumulation—bridge, drift-wood, and ice—would be borne irresistibly down the stream together.

Scipio's bridge, however, answered very well for his purpose. His army passed over it in safety. When Hannibal heard of this, he knew that the battle was at hand. Hannibal was himself at this time about five miles distant. While Scipio was at work upon the bridge, Hannibal was employed, mainly, as he had been all the time since his descent from the mountains, in the subjugation of the various petty nations and tribes north of the Po. Some of them were well disposed to join his standard. Others were allies of the Romans, and wished to remain so. He made treaties and sent help to the former, and dispatched detachments of troops to intimidate and subdue the latter. When, however, he learned that Scipio had crossed the river, he ordered all these detachments to come immediately in, and he began to prepare in earnest for the contest that was impending.

He called together an assembly of his soldiers, and announced to them finally that the battle was now nigh. He renewed the words of encouragement that he had spoken before, and in addition to what he then said, he now promised the soldiers rewards in land in case they proved victorious. "I will give you each a farm," said he, "wherever you choose to have it, either in Africa, Italy, or Spain. If, instead of the land, any of you shall prefer to receive rather an equivalent in money, you shall have the reward in that form, and then you can return home and live with your friends, as before the war, under circumstances which will make you objects of envy to those who remained behind. If any of you would like to live in Carthage, I will have you made free citizens, so that you can live there in independence and honor."

But what security would there be for the faithful fulfillment of these promises? In modern times such security is given by bonds, with pecuniary penalties, or by the deposit of titles to property in responsible hands. In ancient days they managed differently. The promiser bound himself by some solemn and formal mode of adjuration, accompanied, in important cases, with certain ceremonies, which were supposed to seal and confirm the obligation assumed. In this case Hannibal brought a lamb in the presence of the assembled army. He held it before them with his left hand, while with his right he grasped a heavy stone. He then called aloud upon the gods, imploring them to destroy him as he was about to slay the lamb, if he failed to perform faithfully and fully the pledges that he had made. He then struck the poor lamb a heavy blow with the stone. The animal fell dead at his feet, and Hannibal was thenceforth bound, in the opinion of the army, by a very solemn obligation indeed, to be faithful in fulfilling his word.

The soldiers were greatly animated and excited by these promises, and were in haste to have the contest come on. The Roman soldiers, it seems, were in a different mood of mind. Some circumstances had occurred which they considered as bad omens, and they were very much dispirited and depressed by them. It is astonishing that men should ever allow their minds to be affected by such wholly accidental occurrences as these were. One of them was this: a wolf came into their camp, from one of the forests near, and after wounding several men, made his escape again. The other was more trifling still. A swarm of bees flew into the encampment, and lighted upon a tree just over Scipio's tent. This was considered, for some reason or other, a sign that some calamity was going to befall them, and the men were accordingly intimidated and disheartened. They consequently looked forward to the battle with uneasiness and anxiety, while the army of Hannibal anticipated it with eagerness and pleasure.

The battle came on, at last, very suddenly, and at a moment when neither party were expecting it. A large detachment of both armies were advancing toward the position of the other, near the River Ticinus, to reconnoiter, when they met, and the battle began. Hannibal advanced with great impetuosity, and sent, at the same time, a detachment around to attack his enemy in the rear. The Romans soon began to fall into confusion; the horsemen and foot soldiers got entangled together; the men were trampled upon by the horses, and the horses were frightened by the men. In the midst of this scene, Scipio received a wound. A consul was a dignitary of very high consideration. He was, in fact, a sort of semi-king. The officers, and all the soldiers, so fast as they heard that the consul was wounded, were terrified and dismayed, and the Romans began to retreat. Scipio had a young son, named also Scipio, who was then about twenty years of age. He was fighting by the side of his father when he received his wound. He protected his father, got him into the center of a compact body of cavalry, and moved slowly off the ground, those in the rear facing toward the enemy and beating them back, as they pressed on in pursuit of them. In this way they reached their camp. Here they stopped for the night. They had fortified the place, and, as night was coming on, Hannibal thought it not prudent to press on and attack them there. He waited for the morning. Scipio, however, himself wounded and his army discouraged, thought it not prudent for him to wait till the morning. At midnight he put his whole force in motion on a retreat. He kept the camp-fires burning, and did every thing else in his power to prevent the Carthaginians observing any indications of his departure. His army marched secretly and silently till they reached the river. They recrossed it by the bridge they had built, and then, cutting away the fastenings by which the different rafts were held together, the structure was at once destroyed, and the materials of which it was composed floated away, a mere mass of ruins, down the stream. From the Ticinus they floated, we may imagine, into the Po, and thence down the Po into the Adriatic Sea, where they drifted about upon the waste of waters till they were at last, one after another driven by storms upon the sandy shores.

7

The Apennines

AS soon as Hannibal was apprised in the morning that Scipio and his forces had left their ground, he pressed on after them, very earnest to overtake them before they should reach the river. But he was too late. The main body of the Roman army had got over. There was, however, a detachment of a few hundred men, who had been left on Hannibal's side of the river to guard the bridge until all the army should have passed, and then to help in cutting it away. They had accomplished this before Hannibal's arrival, but had not had time to contrive any way to get across the river themselves. Hannibal took them all prisoners.

The condition and prospects of both the Roman and Carthaginian cause were entirely changed by this battle, and the retreat of Scipio across the Po. All the nations of the north of Italy, who had been subjects or allies of the Romans, now turned to Hannibal. They sent embassies into his camp, offering him their friendship and alliance. In fact, there was a large body of Gauls in the Roman camp, who were fighting under Scipio at the battle of Ticinus, who deserted his standard immediately afterward, and came over in a mass to Hannibal. They made this revolt in the night, and, instead of stealing away secretly, they raised a prodigious tumult, killed the guards, filled the encampment with their shouts and outcries, and created for a time an awful scene of terror.

Hannibal received them, but he was too sagacious to admit such a treacherous horde into his army. He treated them with great consideration and kindness, and dismissed them with presents, that they might all go to their respective homes, charging them to exert their influence in his favor among the tribes to which they severally belonged.

Hannibal's soldiers, too, were very much encouraged by the commencement they had made. The army made immediate preparations for crossing the river. Some of the soldiers built rafts, others went up the stream in search of places to ford. Some swam across. They could adopt these or any other modes in safety, for the Romans made no stand on the opposite bank to oppose them, but moved rapidly on, as fast as Scipio could be carried. His wounds began to inflame, and were extremely painful.

In fact, the Romans were dismayed at the danger which now threatened them. As soon as news of these events reached the city, the authorities there sent a dispatch immediately to Sicily to recall the other consul. His name was Sempronius. It will be recollected that, when the lots were cast between him and Scipio, it fell to Scipio to proceed to Spain, with a view to arresting Hannibal's march, while Sempronius went to Sicily and Africa. The object of this movement was to threaten and attack the Carthaginians at home, in order to distract their attention and prevent their sending any fresh forces to aid Hannibal, and, perhaps, even to compel them to recall him from Italy to defend their own capital. But now that Hannibal had not only passed the Alps, but had also crossed the Po, and was marching toward Rome—Scipio himself disabled, and his army flying before him—they were obliged at once to abandon the plan of threatening Carthage. They sent with all dispatch an order to Sempronius to hasten home and assist in the defense of Rome.

Sempronius was a man of a very prompt and impetuous character, with great confidence in his own powers, and very ready for action. He came immediately into Italy, recruited new soldiers for the army, put himself at the head of his forces, and marched northward to join Scipio in the valley of the Po. Scipio was suffering great pain from his wounds, and could do but little toward directing the operations of the army. He had slowly retreated before Hannibal, the fever and pain of his wounds being greatly exasperated by the motion of traveling. In this manner he arrived at the Trebia, a small stream flowing northward into the Po. He crossed this stream, and finding that he could not go any further, on account of the torturing pain to which it put him to be moved, he halted his army, marked out an encampment, threw up fortifications around it, and prepared to make a stand. To his great relief, Sempronius soon came up and joined him here.

There were now two generals. Napoleon used to say that one bad commander was better than two good ones, so essential is it to success in all military operations to secure that promptness, and confidence, and decision which can only exist where action is directed by one single mind. Sempronius and Scipio disagreed as to the proper course to be pursued. Sempronius wished to attack Hannibal immediately. Scipio was in favor of delay. Sempronius attributed Scipio's reluctance to give battle to the dejection of mind and discouragement produced by his wound, or to a feeling of envy lest he, Sempronius, should have the honor of conquering the Carthaginians, while he himself was helpless in his tent. On the other hand, Scipio thought Sempronius inconsiderate and reckless; and disposed to rush heedlessly into a contest with a foe whose powers and resources he did not understand.

In the mean time, while the two commanders were thus divided in opinion, some skirmishes and small engagements took place between detachments from the two armies, in which Sempronius thought that the Romans had the advantage. This excited his enthusiasm more and more, and he became extremely desirous to bring on a general battle. He began to be quite out of patience with Scipio's caution and delay. The soldiers, he said, were full of strength and courage, all eager for the combat, and it was absurd to hold them back on account of the feebleness of one sick man. "Besides," said he, "of what use can it be to delay any longer? We are as ready to meet the Carthaginians now as we shall ever be. There is no third consul to come and help us; and what a disgrace it is for us Romans, who in the former war led our troops to the very gates of Carthage, to allow Hannibal to bear sway over all the north of Italy, while we retreat gradually before him, afraid to encounter now a force that we have always conquered before."

Hannibal was not long in learning, through his spies, that there was this difference of opinion between the Roman generals, and that Sempronius was full of a presumptuous sort of ardor, and he began to think that he could contrive some plan to draw the latter out into battle under circumstances in which he would have to act at a great disadvantage. He did contrive such a plan. It succeeded admirably; and the case was one of those numerous instances which occurred in the history of Hannibal, of successful stratagem, which led the Romans to say that his leading traits of character were treachery and cunning.

Hannibal's plan was, in a word, an attempt to draw the Roman army out of its encampment on a dark, cold, and stormy night in December, and get them into the river. This river was the Trebia. It flowed north into the Po, between the Roman and Carthaginian camps. His scheme, in detail, was to send a part of his army over the river to attack the Romans in the night or very early in the morning. He hoped that by this means Sempronius would be induced to come out of his camp to attack the Carthaginians. The Carthaginians were then to fly and recross the river, and Hannibal hoped that Sempronius would follow, excited by the ardor of pursuit. Hannibal was then to have a strong reserve of the army, that had remained all the time in warmth and safety, to come out and attack the Romans with unimpaired strength and vigor, while the Romans themselves would be benumbed by the cold and wet, and disorganized by the confusion produced in crossing the stream.

A part of Hannibal's reserve were to be placed in an ambuscade. There were some meadows near the water, which were covered in many places with tall grass and bushes. Hannibal went to examine the spot, and found that this shrubbery was high enough for even horsemen to be concealed in it. He determined to place a thousand foot soldiers and a thousand horsemen here, the most efficient and courageous in the army. He selected them in the following manner:

He called one of his lieutenant generals to the spot, explained somewhat of his design to him, and then asked him to go and choose from the cavalry and the infantry, a hundred each, the best soldiers he could find. This two hundred were then assembled, and Hannibal, after surveying them with looks of approbation and pleasure, said, "Yes, you are the men I want, only, instead of two hundred, I need two thousand. Go back to the army, and select and bring to me, each of you, nine men like yourselves." It is easy to be imagined that the soldiers were pleased with this commission, and that they executed it faithfully. The whole force thus chosen was soon assembled, and stationed in the thickets above described, where they lay in ambush ready to attack the Romans after they should pass the river.

Hannibal also made arrangements for leaving a large part of his army in his own camp, ready for battle, with orders that they should partake of food and refreshments, and keep themselves warm by the fires until they should be called upon. All things being thus ready, he detached a body of horsemen to cross the river, and see if they could provoke the Romans to come out of their camp and pursue them.

"Go," said Hannibal, to the commander of this detachment, "pass the stream, advance to the Roman camp, assail the guards, and when the army forms and comes out to attack you, retreat slowly before them back across the river."

The detachment did as it was ordered to do. When they arrived at the camp, which was soon after break of day—for it was a part of Hannibal's plan to bring the Romans out before they should have had time to breakfast—Sempronius, at the first alarm, called all the soldiers to arms, supposing that the whole Carthaginian force was attacking them. It was a cold and stormy morning, and the atmosphere being filled with rain and snow, but little could be seen. Column after column of horsemen and of infantry marched out of the camp. The Carthaginians retreated. Sempronius was greatly excited at the idea of so easily driving back the assailants, and, as they retreated, he pressed on in pursuit of them. As Hannibal had anticipated, he became so excited in the pursuit that he did not stop at the banks of the river. The Carthaginian horsemen plunged into the stream in their retreat, and the Romans, foot soldiers and horsemen together, followed on. The stream was usually small, but it was now swelled by the rain which had been falling all the night. The water was, of course, intensely cold. The horsemen got through tolerably well, but the foot soldiers were all thoroughly drenched and benumbed; and as they had not taken any food that morning, and had come forth on a very sudden call, and without any sufficient preparation, they felt the effects of the exposure in the strongest degree. Still they pressed on. They ascended the bank after crossing the river, and when they had formed again there, and were moving forward in pursuit of their still flying enemy, suddenly the whole force of Hannibal's reserves, strong and vigorous, just from their tent and their fires, burst upon them. They had scarcely recovered from the astonishment and the shock of this unexpected onset, when the two thousand concealed in the ambuscade came sallying forth in the storm, and assailed the Romans in the rear with frightful shouts and outcries.

All these movements took place very rapidly. Only a very short period elapsed from the time that the Roman army, officers and soldiers, were quietly sleeping in their camp, or rising slowly to prepare for the routine of an ordinary day, before they found themselves all drawn out in battle array some miles from their encampment, and surrounded and hemmed in by their foes. The events succeeded each other so rapidly as to appear to the soldiers like a dream; but very soon their wet and freezing clothes, their limbs benumbed and stiffened, the sleet which was driving along the plain, the endless lines of Carthaginian infantry, hemming them in on all sides, and the columns of horsemen and of elephants charging upon them, convinced them that their situation was one of dreadful reality. The calamity, too, which threatened them was of vast extent, as well as imminent and terrible; for, though the stratagem of Hannibal was very simple in its plan and management, still he had executed it on a great scale, and had brought out the whole Roman army. There were, it is said, about forty thousand that crossed the river, and about an equal number in the Carthaginian army to oppose them. Such a body of combatants covered, of course, a large extent of ground, and the conflict that ensued was one of the most horrible scenes of the many that Hannibal assisted in enacting.

The conflict continued for many hours, the Romans getting more and more into confusion all the time. The elephants of the Carthaginians, that is, the few that now remained, made great havoc in their ranks, and finally, after a combat of some hours, the whole army was broken up and fled, some portions in compact bodies, as their officers could keep them together, and others in hopeless and inextricable confusion. They made their way back to the river, which they reached at various points up and down the stream. In the mean time, the continued rain had swollen the waters still more, the low lands were overflowed, the deep places concealed, and the broad expanse of water in the center of the stream whirled in boiling and turbid eddies, whose surface was roughened by the December breeze, and dotted every where with the drops of rain still falling.

When the Roman army was thoroughly broken up and scattered, the Carthaginians gave up the further prosecution of the contest. They were too wet, cold, and exhausted themselves to feel any ardor in the pursuit of their enemies. Vast numbers of the Romans, however, attempted to recross the river, and were swept down and destroyed by the merciless flood, whose force they had not strength enough remaining to withstand. Other portions of the troops lay hid in lurking-places to which they had retreated, until night came on, and then they made rafts on which they contrived to float themselves back across the stream. Hannibal's troops were too wet, and cold, and exhausted to go out again into the storm, and so they were unmolested in these attempts. Notwithstanding this, however, great numbers of them were carried down the stream and lost.

It was now December, too late for Hannibal to attempt to advance much further that season, and yet the way before him was open to the Apennines, by the defeat of Sempronius, for neither he nor Scipio could now hope to make another stand against him till they should receive new re-enforcements from Rome. During the winter months Hannibal had various battles and adventures, sometimes with portions and detachments of the Roman army, and sometimes with the native tribes. He was sometimes in great difficulty for want of food for his army, until at length he bribed the governor of a castle, where a Roman granary was kept, to deliver it up to him, and after that he was well supplied.

The natives of the country were, however, not at all well disposed toward him, and in the course of the winter they attempted to impede his operations, and to harass his army by every means in their power. Finding his situation uncomfortable, he moved on toward the south, and at length determined that, inclement as the season was, he would cross the Apennines.

By looking at the map of Italy, it will be seen that the great valley of the Po extends across the whole north of Italy. The valley of the Arno and of the Umbro lies south of it, separated from it by a part of the Apennine chain. This southern valley was Etruria. Hannibal decided to attempt to pass over the mountains into Etruria. He thought he should find there a warmer climate, and inhabitants more well-disposed toward him, besides being so much nearer Rome.

But, though Hannibal conquered the Alps, the Apennines conquered him. A very violent storm arose just as he reached the most exposed place among the mountains. It was intensely cold, and the wind blew the hail and snow directly into the faces of the troops, so that it was impossible for them to proceed. They halted and turned their backs to the storm, but the wind increased more and more, and was attended with terrific thunder and lightning, which filled the soldiers with alarm, as they were at such an altitude as to be themselves enveloped in the clouds from which the peals and flashes were emitted. Unwilling to retreat, Hannibal ordered the army to encamp on the spot, in the best shelter they could find. They attempted, accordingly, to pitch their tents, but it was impossible to secure them. The wind increased to a hurricane. The tent poles were unmanageable, and the canvas was carried away from its fastenings, and sometimes split or blown into rags by its flapping in the wind. The poor elephants, that is, all that were left of them from previous battles and exposures, sunk down under this intense cold and died. One only remained alive.

Hannibal ordered a retreat, and the army went back into the valley of the Po. But Hannibal was ill at ease here. The natives of the country were very weary of his presence. His army consumed their food, ravaged their country, and destroyed all their peace and happiness. Hannibal suspected them of a design to poison him or assassinate him in some other way. He was continually watching and taking precautions against these attempts. He had a great many different dresses made to be used as disguises, and false hair of different colors and fashion, so that he could alter his appearance at pleasure. This was to prevent any spy or assassin who might come into his camp from identifying him by any description of his dress and appearance. Still, notwithstanding these precautions, he was ill at ease, and at the very earliest practicable period in the spring he made a new attempt to cross the mountains, and was now successful.

On descending the southern declivities of the Apennines he learned that a new Roman army, under a new consul, was advancing toward him from the south. He was eager to meet this force, and was preparing to press forward at once by the nearest way. He found, however, that this would lead him across the lower part of the valley of the Arno, which was here very broad, and, though usually passable, was now overflowed in consequence of the swelling of the waters of the river by the melting of the snows upon the mountains. The whole country was now, in fact, a vast expanse of marshes and fens.

JACOB ABBOTT

Crossing the Marshes.

Still, Hannibal concluded to cross it, and, in the attempt, he involved his army in difficulties and dangers as great, almost, as he had encountered upon the Alps. The waters were rising continually; they filled all the channels and spread over extended plains. They were so turbid, too, that every thing beneath the surface was concealed, and the soldiers wading in them were continually sinking into deep and sudden channels and into bogs of mire, where many were lost. They were all exhausted and worn out by the wet and cold, and the long continuance of their exposure to it. They were four days and three nights in this situation, as their progress was, of course, extremely slow. The men, during all this time, had scarcely any sleep, and in some places the only way by which they could get any repose was to lay their arms and their baggage in the standing water, so as to build, by this means, a sort of couch or platform on which they could lie. Hannibal himself was sick too. He was attacked with a violent inflammation of the eyes, and the sight of one of them was in the end destroyed. He was not, however, so much exposed as the other officers; for there was one elephant left of all those that had commenced the march in Spain, and Hannibal rode this elephant during the four days' march through the water. There were guides and attendants to precede him, for the purpose of finding a safe and practicable road, and by their aid, with the help of the animal's sagacity, he got safely through.

8

The Dictator Fabius

IN the mean time, while Hannibal was thus rapidly making his way toward the gates of Rome, the people of the city became more and more alarmed, until at last a general feeling or terror pervaded all the ranks of society. Citizens and soldiers were struck with one common dread. They had raised a new army and put it under the command of a new consul, for the terms of service of the others had expired; Flaminius was the name of this new commander, and he was moving northward at the head of his forces at the time that Hannibal was conducting his troops with so much labor and difficulty through the meadows and morasses of the Arno.

This army was, however, no more successful than its predecessors had been. Hannibal contrived to entrap Flaminius by a stratagem, as he had entrapped Sempronius before. There is in the eastern part of Etruria, near the mountains, a lake called Lake Thrasymene. It happened that this lake extended so near to the base of the mountains as to leave only a narrow passage between—a passage but little wider than was necessary for a road. Hannibal contrived to station a detachment of his troops in ambuscade at the foot of the mountains, and others on the declivities above, and then in some way or other to entice Flaminius and his army through the defile. Flaminius was, like Sempronius, ardent, self-confident, and vain. He despised the power of Hannibal, and thought that his success hitherto had been owing to the inefficiency or indecision of his predecessors. For his part, his only anxiety was to encounter him, for he was sure of an easy victory. He advanced, therefore, boldly and without concern into the pass of Thrasymene, when he learned that Hannibal was encamped beyond it.

Hannibal had established an encampment openly on some elevated ground beyond the pass, and as Flaminius and his troops came into the narrowest part of the defile, they saw this encampment at a distance before them, with a broad plain beyond the pass intervening. They supposed that the whole force of the enemy was there, not dreaming of the presence of the strong detachments which were hid on the slopes of the mountains above them, and were looking down upon them at that very moment from behind rocks and bushes. When, therefore, the Romans had got through the pass, they spread out upon the plain beyond it, and were advancing to the camp, when suddenly the secreted troops burst forth from their ambuscade, and, pouring down the mountains, took complete possession of the pass, and attacked the Romans in the rear, while Hannibal attacked them in the van. Another long, and desperate, and bloody contest ensued. The Romans were beaten at every point, and, as they were hemmed in between the lake, the mountain, and the pass, they could not retreat; the army was, accordingly, almost wholly cut to pieces. Flaminius himself was killed.

The news of this battle spread every where, and produced the strongest sensation. Hannibal sent dispatches to Carthage announcing what he considered his final victory over the great foe, and the news was received with the greatest rejoicings. At Rome, on the other hand, the news produced a dreadful shock of disappointment and terror. It seemed as if the last hope of resisting the progress of their terrible enemy was gone, and that they had nothing now to do but to sink down in despair, and await the hour when his columns should come pouring in through the gates of the city.

The people of Rome were, in fact, prepared for a panic, for their fears had been increasing and gathering strength for some time. They were very superstitious in those ancient days in respect to signs and omens. A thousand trifling occurrences, which would, at the present day, be considered of no consequence whatever, were then considered bad signs, auguring terrible calamities; and, on occasions like these, when calamities seemed to be impending, every thing was noticed, and circumstances which would not have been regarded at all at ordinary times, were reported from one to another, the stories being exaggerated as they spread, until the imaginations of the people were filled with mysterious but invincible fears. So universal was the belief in these prodigies and omens, that they were sometimes formally reported to the senate, committees were appointed to inquire into them, and solemn sacrifices were offered to "expiate them," as it was termed, that is, to avert the displeasure of the gods, which the omens were supposed to foreshadow and portend.

A very curious list of these omens was reported to the senate during the winter and spring in which Hannibal was advancing toward Rome. An ox from the cattle-market had got into a house, and, losing his way, had climbed up into the third story, and, being frightened by the noise and uproar of those who followed him, ran out of a window and fell down to the ground. A light appeared in the sky in the form of ships. A temple was struck with lightning. A spear in the hand of a statue of Juno, a celebrated goddess, shook, one day, of itself. Apparitions of men in white garments were seen in a certain place. A wolf came into a camp, and snatched the sword of a soldier on guard out of his hands, and ran away with it. The sun one day looked smaller than usual. Two moons were seen together in the sky. This was in the daytime, and one of the moons was doubtless a halo or a white cloud. Stones fell out of the sky at a place called Picenum. This was one of the most dreadful of all the omens, though it is now known to be a common occurrence.

These omens were all, doubtless, real occurrences, more or less remarkable, it is true, but, of course, entirely unmeaning in respect to their being indications of impending calamities. There were other things reported to the senate which must have originated almost wholly in the imaginations and fears of the observers. Two shields, it was said, in a certain camp, sweat blood. Some people were reaping, and bloody ears of grain fell into the basket. This, of course, must have been wholly imaginary, unless, indeed, one of the reapers had cut his fingers with the sickle. Some streams and fountains became bloody; and, finally, in one place in the country, some goats turned into sheep. A hen, also, became a cock, and a cock changed to a hen.

Such ridiculous stories would not be worthy of a moment's attention now, were it not for the degree of importance attached to them then. They were formally reported to the Roman senate, the witnesses who asserted that they had seen them were called in and examined, and a solemn debate was held on the question what should be done to avert the supernatural influences of evil which the omens expressed. The senate decided to have three days of expiation and sacrifice, during which the whole people of Rome devoted themselves to the religious observances which they thought calculated to appease the wrath of Heaven. They made various offerings and gifts to the different gods, among which one was a golden thunderbolt of fifty pounds' weight, manufactured for Jupiter, whom they considered the thunderer.

All these things took place before the battle at Lake Thrasymene, so that the whole community were in a very feverish state of excitement and anxiety before the news from Flaminius arrived. When these tidings at last came, they threw the whole city into utter consternation. Of course, the messenger went directly to the senate-house to report to the government, but the story that such news had arrived soon spread about the city, and the whole population crowded into the streets and public squares, all eagerly asking for the tidings. An enormous throng assembled before the senate-house calling for information. A public officer appeared at last, and said to them in a loud voice, "We have been defeated in a great battle." He would say no more. Still rumors spread from one to another, until it was generally known throughout the city that Hannibal had conquered the Roman army again in a great battle, that great numbers of the soldiers had fallen or been taken prisoners, and that the consul himself was slain.

The night was passed in great anxiety and terror, and the next day, and for several of the succeeding days, the people gathered in great numbers around the gates, inquiring eagerly for news of every one that came in from the country. Pretty soon scattered soldiers and small bodies of troops began to arrive, bringing with them information of the battle, each one having a different tale to tell, according to his own individual experience in the scene. Whenever these men arrived, the people of the city, and especially the women who had husbands or sons in the army, crowded around them, overwhelming them with questions, and making them tell their tale again and again, as if the intolerable suspense and anxiety of the hearers could not be satisfied. The intelligence was such as in general to confirm and increase the fears of those who listened to it; but sometimes, when it made known the safety of a husband or a son, it produced as much relief and rejoicing as it did in other cases terror and despair. That maternal love was as strong an impulse in those rough days as it is in the more refined and cultivated periods of the present age, is evinced by the fact that two of these Roman mothers, on seeing their sons coming suddenly into their presence, alive and well, when they had heard that they had fallen in battle, were killed at once by the shock of surprise and joy, as if by a blow.

In seasons of great and imminent danger to the commonwealth, it was the custom of the Romans to appoint what they called a dictator, that is, a supreme executive, who was clothed with absolute and unlimited powers; and it devolved on him to save the state from the threatened ruin by the most prompt and energetic action. This case was obviously one of the emergencies requiring such a measure. There was no time for deliberations and debates; for deliberations and debates, in periods of such excitement and danger, become disputes, and end in tumult and uproar. Hannibal was at the head of a victorious army, ravaging the country which he had already conquered, and with no obstacle between him, and the city itself. It was an emergency calling for the appointment of a dictator. The people made choice of a man of great reputation for experience and wisdom, named Fabius, and placed the whole power of the state in his hands. All other authority was suspended, and every thing was subjected to his sway. The whole city, with the life and property of every inhabitant, was placed at his disposal; the army and the fleets were also under his command, even the consuls being subject to his orders.

Fabius accepted the vast responsibility which his election imposed upon him, and immediately began to take the necessary measures. He first made arrangements for performing solemn religious ceremonies, to expiate the omens and propitiate the gods. He brought out all the people in great convocations, and made them take vows, in the most formal and imposing manner, promising offerings and celebrations in honor of the various gods, at some future time, in case these divinities would avert the threatening danger. It is doubtful, however, whether Fabius, in doing these things, really believed that they had any actual efficiency, or whether he resorted to them as a means of calming and quieting the minds of the people, and producing that composure and confidence which always results from a hope of the favor of Heaven. If this last was his object, his conduct was eminently wise.

Fabius, also, immediately ordered a large levy of troops to be made. His second in command, called his master of horse, was directed to make this levy, and to assemble the troops at a place called Tibur, a few miles east of the city. There was always a master of horse appointed to attend upon and second a dictator. The name of this officer in the case of Fabius was Minucius. Minucius was as ardent, prompt, and impetuous, as Fabius was cool, prudent, and calculating. He levied the troops and brought them to their place of rendezvous. Fabius went out to take the command of them. One of the consuls was coming to join him, with a body of troops which he had under his command. Fabius sent word to him that he must come without any of the insignia of his authority, as all his authority, semi-regal as it was in ordinary times, was superseded and overruled in the presence of a dictator. A consul was accustomed to move in great state on all occasions. He was preceded by twelve men, bearing badges and insignia, to impress the army and the people with a sense of the greatness of his dignity. To see, therefore, a consul divested of all these marks of his power, and coming into the dictator's presence as any other officer would come before an acknowledged superior, made the army of Fabius feel a very strong sense of the greatness of their new commander's dignity and power.

Fabius then issued a proclamation, which he sent by proper messengers into all the region of country around Rome, especially to that part toward the territory which was in possession of Hannibal. In this proclamation he ordered all the people to abandon the country and the towns which were not strongly fortified, and to seek shelter in the castles, and forts, and fortified cities. They were commanded, also, to lay waste the country which they should leave, and destroy all the property, and especially all the provisions, which they could not take to their places of refuge. This being done, Fabius placed himself at the head of the forces which he had got together, and moved on, cautiously and with great circumspection, in search of his enemy.

In the mean time, Hannibal had crossed over to the eastern side of Italy, and had passed down, conquering and ravaging the country as he went, until he got considerably south of Rome. He seems to have thought it not quite prudent to advance to the actual attack of the city, after the battle of Lake Thrasymene; for the vast population of Rome was sufficient, if rendered desperate by his actually threatening the capture and pillage of the city, to overwhelm his army entirely. So he moved to the eastward, and advanced on that side until he had passed the city, and thus it happened that Fabius had to march to the southward and eastward in order to meet him. The two armies came in sight of each other quite on the eastern side of Italy, very near the shores of the Adriatic Sea.

The policy which Fabius resolved to adopt was, not to give Hannibal battle, but to watch him, and wear his army out by fatigue and delays. He kept, therefore, near him, but always posted his army on advantageous ground, which all the defiance and provocations of Hannibal could not induce him to leave. When Hannibal moved, which he was soon compelled to do to procure provisions, Fabius would move too, but only to post and intrench himself in some place of security as before. Hannibal did every thing in his power to bring Fabius to battle, but all his efforts were unavailing.

In fact, he himself was at one time in imminent danger. He had got drawn, by Fabius's good management, into a place where he was surrounded by mountains, upon which Fabius had posted his troops, and there was only one defile which offered any egress, and this, too, Fabius had strongly guarded. Hannibal resorted to his usual resource, cunning and stratagem, for means of escape. He collected a herd of oxen. He tied fagots across their horns, filling the fagots with pitch, so as to make them highly combustible. In the night on which he was going to attempt to pass the defile, he ordered his army to be ready to march through, and then had the oxen driven up the hills around on the further side of the Roman detachment which was guarding the pass. The fagots were then lighted on the horns of the oxen. They ran about, frightened and infuriated by the fire, which burned their horns to the quick, and blinded them with the sparks which fell from it. The leaves and branches of the forests were set on fire. A great commotion was thus made, and the guards, seeing the moving lights and hearing the tumult, supposed that the Carthaginian army were upon the heights, and were coming down to attack them. They turned out in great hurry and confusion to meet the imaginary foe, leaving the pass unguarded, and, while they were pursuing the bonfires on the oxen's heads into all sorts of dangerous and impracticable places, Hannibal quietly marched his army through the defile and reached a place of safety.

Although Fabius kept Hannibal employed and prevented his approaching the city, still there soon began to be felt a considerable degree of dissatisfaction that he did not act more decidedly. Minucius was continually urging him to give Hannibal battle, and, not being able to induce him to do so; he was continually expressing his discontent and displeasure. The army sympathized with Minucius. He wrote home to Rome too, complaining bitterly of the dictator's inefficiency. Hannibal learned all this by means of his spies, and other sources of information, which so good a contriver as he has always at command. Hannibal was, of course, very much pleased to hear of these dissensions, and of the unpopularity of Fabius. He considered such an enemy as he—so prudent, cautious, and watchful—as a far more dangerous foe than such bold and impetuous commanders as Flaminius and Minucius, whom he could always entice into difficulty, and then easily conquer.

Hannibal thought he would render Minucius a little help in making Fabius unpopular. He found out from Roman deserters that the dictator possessed a valuable farm in the country, and he sent a detachment of his troops there, with orders to plunder and destroy the property all around it, but to leave the farm of Fabius untouched and in safety. The object was to give to the enemies of Fabius at Rome occasion to say that there was secretly a good understanding between him and Hannibal, and that he was kept back from acting boldly in defense of his country by some corrupt bargain which he had traitorously made with the enemy.

These plans succeeded. Discontent and dissatisfaction spread rapidly, both in the camp and in the city. At Rome they made an urgent demand upon Fabius to return, ostensibly because they wished him to take part in some great religious ceremonies, but really to remove him from the camp, and give Minucius an opportunity to attack Hannibal. They also wished to devise some method, if possible, of depriving him of his power. He had been appointed for six months, and the time had not yet nearly expired; but they wished to shorten, or, if they could not shorten, to limit and diminish his power.

Fabius went to Rome, leaving the army under the orders of Minucius, but commanding him positively not to give Hannibal battle; nor expose his troops to any danger, but to pursue steadily the same policy which he himself had followed. He had, however, been in Rome only a short time before tidings came that Minucius had fought a battle and gained a victory. There were boastful and ostentatious letters from Minucius to the Roman senate, lauding the exploit which he had performed.

Fabius examined carefully the accounts. He compared one thing with another, and satisfied himself of what afterward proved to be the truth, that Minucius had gained no victory at all. He had lost five or six thousand men, and Hannibal had lost no more, and Fabius showed that no advantage had been gained. He urged upon the senate the importance of adhering to the line of policy he had pursued, and the danger of risking every thing, as Minucius had done, on the fortunes of a single battle. Besides, he said, Minucius had disobeyed his orders, which were distinct and positive, and he deserved to be recalled.

In saying these things Fabius irritated and exasperated his enemies more than ever. "Here is a man," said they, "who will not only not fight the enemies whom he is sent against himself, but he will not allow any body else to fight them. Even at this distance, when his second in command has obtained a victory, he will not admit it, and endeavors to curtail the advantages of it. He wishes to protract the war, that he may the longer continue to enjoy the supreme and unlimited authority with which we have entrusted him."

The hostility to Fabius at last reached such a pitch, that it was proposed in an assembly of the people to make Minucius his equal in command. Fabius, having finished the business which called him to Rome, did not wait to attend to the discussion of this question, but left the city, and was proceeding on his way to join the army again, when he was overtaken with a messenger bearing a letter informing him that the decree had passed, and that he must thenceforth consider Minucius as his colleague and equal. Minucius was, of course, extremely elated at this result. "Now," said he, "we will see if something can not be done."

The first question was, however, to decide on what principle and in what way they should share their power. "We can not both command at once," said Minucius. "Let us exercise the power in alternation, each one being in authority for a day, or a week, or a month, or any other period that you prefer."

"No," replied Fabius, "we will not divide the time, we will divide the men. There are four legions. You shall take two of them, and the other two shall be mine. I can thus, perhaps, save half the army from the dangers in which I fear your impetuosity will plunge all whom you have under your command."

This plan was adopted. The army was divided, and each portion went, under its own leader, to its separate encampment. The result was one of the most curious and extraordinary occurrences that is recorded in the history of nations. Hannibal, who was well informed of all these transactions, immediately felt that Minucius was in his power. He knew that he was so eager for battle that it would be easy to entice him into it, under almost any circumstances that he himself might choose to arrange. Accordingly, he watched his opportunity when there was a good place for an ambuscade near Minucius's camp, and lodged five thousand men in it in such a manner that they were concealed by rocks and other obstructions to the view. There was a hill between this ground and the camp of Minucius. When the ambuscade was ready, Hannibal sent up a small force to take possession of the top of the hill anticipating that Minucius would at once send up a stronger force to drive them away. He did so. Hannibal then sent up more as a re-enforcement. Minucius, whose spirit and pride were now aroused, sent up more still, and thus, by degrees, Hannibal drew out his enemy's whole force, and then, ordering his own troops to retreat before them, the Romans were drawn on, down the hill, till they were surrounded by the ambuscade. These hidden troops then came pouring out upon them, and in a short time the Romans were thrown into utter confusion, flying in all directions before their enemies, and entirely at their mercy.

All would have been irretrievably lost had it not been for the interposition of Fabius. He received intelligence of the danger at his own camp, and marched out at once with all his force, and arrived upon the ground so opportunely, and acted so efficiently, that he at once completely changed the fortune of the day. He saved Minucius and his half of the army from utter destruction. The Carthaginians retreated in their turn, Hannibal being entirely overwhelmed with disappointment and vexation at being thus deprived of his prey. History relates that

Minucius had the candor and good sense, after this, to acknowledge his error, and yield to the guidance and direction of Fabius. He called his part of the army together when they reached their camp, and addressed them thus: "Fellow-soldiers, I have often heard it said that the wisest men are those who possess wisdom and sagacity themselves, and, next to them, those who know how to perceive and are willing to be guided by the wisdom and sagacity of others; while they are fools who do not know how to conduct themselves, and will not be guided by those who do. We will not belong to this last class; and since it is proved that we are not entitled to rank with the first, let us join the second. We will march to the camp of Fabius, and join our camp with his, as before. We owe to him, and also to all his portion of the army, our eternal gratitude for the nobleness of spirit which he manifested in coming to our deliverance, when he might so justly have left us to ourselves."

The two legions repaired, accordingly, to the camp of Fabius, and a complete and permanent reconciliation took place between the two divisions of the army. Fabius rose very high in the general esteem by this transaction. The term of his dictatorship, however, expired soon after this, and as the danger from Hannibal was now less imminent, the office was not renewed, but consuls were chosen as before.

The character of Fabius has been regarded with the highest admiration by all mankind. He evinced a very noble spirit in all that he did. One of his last acts was a very striking proof of this. He had bargained with Hannibal to pay a certain sum of money as ransom for a number of prisoners which had fallen into his hands, and whom Hannibal, on the faith of that promise, had released. Fabius believed that the Romans would readily ratify the treaty and pay the amount; but they demurred, being displeased, or pretending to be displeased, because Fabius had not consulted them before making the arrangement. Fabius, in order to preserve his own and his country's faith unsullied, sold his farm to raise the money. He did thus most certainly protect and vindicate his own honor, but he can hardly be said to have saved that of the people of Rome.

9

The Battle of Cannæ

THE battle of Cannæ was the last great battle fought by Hannibal in Italy. This conflict has been greatly celebrated in history, not only for its magnitude, and the terrible desperation with which it was fought, but also on account of the strong dramatic interest which the circumstances attending it are fitted to excite. This interest is perhaps, however, quite as much due to the peculiar skill of the ancient historian who narrates the story, as to the events themselves which he records.

It was about a year after the close of the dictatorship of Fabius that this battle was fought. That interval had been spent by the Roman consuls who were in office during that time in various military operations, which did not, however, lead to any decisive results. In the mean time, there were great uneasiness, discontent, and dissatisfaction at Rome. To have such a dangerous and terrible foe, at the head of forty thousand men, infesting the vicinage of their city, ravaging the territories of their friends and allies, and threatening continually to attack the city itself, was a continual source of anxiety and vexation. It mortified the Roman pride, too, to find that the greatest armies they could raise, and the ablest generals they could choose and commission, proved wholly unable to cope with the foe. The most sagacious of them, in fact, had felt it necessary to decline the contest with him altogether.

This state of things produced a great deal of ill humor in the city. Party spirit ran very high; tumultuous assemblies were held; disputes and contentions prevailed, and mutual criminations and recriminations without end. There were two great parties formed: that of the middling classes on one side, and the aristocracy on the other. The former were called the Plebeians, the latter the Patricians. The division between these two classes was very great and very strongly marked. There was, in consequence of it, infinite difficulty in the election of consuls. At last the consuls were chosen, one from each party. The name of the patrician was Paulus Æmilius. The name of the plebeian was Varro. They were inducted into office and were thus put jointly into possession of a vast power, to wield which with any efficiency and success would seem to require union and harmony in those who held it, and yet Æmilius and Varro were inveterate and implacable political foes. It was often so in the Roman government. The consulship was a double-headed monster, which spent half its strength in bitter contests waged between its members.

The Romans determined now to make an effectual effort to rid themselves of their foe. They raised an enormous army. It consisted of eight legions. The Roman legion was an army of itself. It contained ordinarily four thousand foot soldiers, and a troop of three hundred horsemen. It was very unusual to have more than two or three legions in the field at a time. The Romans, however, on this occasion, increased the number of the legions, and also augmented their size, so that they contained, each, five thousand infantry and four hundred cavalry. They were determined to make a great and last effort to defend their city, and save the commonwealth from ruin. Æmilius and Varro prepared to take command of this great force, with very strong determinations to make it the means of Hannibal's destruction.

The characters of the two commanders, however, as well as their political connections, were very dissimilar, and they soon began to manifest a very different spirit, and to assume a very different air and bearing, each from the other. Æmilius was a friend of Fabius, and approved of his policy. Varro was for greater promptness and decision. He made great promises, and spoke with the utmost confidence of being able to annihilate Hannibal at a blow. He condemned the policy of Fabius in attempting to wear out the enemy by delays. He said it was a plan of the aristocratic party to protract the war, in order to put themselves in high offices, and perpetuate their importance and influence. The war might have been ended long ago, he said; and he would promise the people that he would now end it, without fail, the very day that he came in sight of Hannibal.

As for Æmilius, he assumed a very different tone. He was surprised, he said, that any man could pretend to decide before he had even left the city, and while he was, of course entirely ignorant, both of the condition of their own army, and of the position, and designs, and strength of the enemy, how soon and under what circumstances it would be wise to give him battle. Plans must be formed in adaptation to circumstances, as circumstances can not be made to alter to suit plans. He believed that they should succeed in the encounter with Hannibal, but he thought that their only hope of success must be based on the exercise of prudence, caution, and sagacity; he was sure that rashness and folly could only lead in future, as they had always done in the past, to discomfiture and ruin.

It is said that Fabius, the former dictator, conversed with Æmilius before his departure for the army, and gave him such counsel as his age and experience, and his knowledge of the character and operation of Hannibal, suggested to his mind. "If you had a colleague like yourself," said he, "I would not offer you any advice; you would not need it. Or, if you were yourself like your colleague, vain, self-conceited, and presumptuous, then I would be silent; counsel would be thrown away upon you. But as it is, while you have great judgment and sagacity to guide you, you are to be placed in a situation of extreme difficulty and peril. If I am not mistaken, the greatest difficulty you will have to encounter will not be the open enemy you are going to meet upon the field. You will find, I think, that Varro will give you quite as much trouble as Hannibal. He will be presumptuous, reckless, and head strong. He will inspire all the rash and ardent young men in the army with his own enthusiastic folly, and we shall be very fortunate if we do not yet see the terrible and bloody scenes of Lake Thrasymene acted again. I am sure that the true policy for us to adopt is the case which I marked out. That is always the proper course for the invaded to pursue with invaders, where there is the least doubt of the success of a battle. We grow strong while Hannibal grows continually weaker by delay. He can only prosper so long as he can fight battles and perform brilliant exploits. If we deprive him of this power, his strength will be continually wasting away, and the spirit and courage of his men waning. He has now scarce a third part of the army which he had when he crossed the Iberus, and nothing can save this remnant from destruction if we are wise."

Æmilius said, in reply to this, that he went into the contest with very little of encouragement or hope. If Fabius had found it so difficult to withstand the turbulent influences of his master of horse, who was his subordinate officer, and, as such, under his command, how could he expect to restrain his colleague, who was entitled by his office, to full equality with him. But, notwithstanding the difficulties which he foresaw, he was going to do his duty, and abide by the result; and if the result should be unfavorable, he should seek for death in the conflict, for death by Carthaginian spears was a far lighter evil, in his view, than the displeasure and censures of his countrymen.

The consuls departed from Rome to join the army, Æmilius attended by a moderate number of men of rank and station, and Varro by a much larger train, though it was formed of people of the lower classes of society. The army was organized, and the arrangements of the encampments perfected. One ceremony was that of administering an oath to the soldiers, as was usual in the Roman armies at the commencement of a campaign. They were made to swear that they would not desert the army, that they would never abandon the post at which they were stationed in fear or in flight, nor leave the ranks except for the purpose of taking up or recovering a weapon, striking an enemy, or protecting a friend. These and other arrangements being completed, the army was ready for the field. The consuls made a different arrangement in respect to the division of their power from that adopted by Fabius and Flaminius. It was agreed between them that they would exercise their common authority alternately, each for a day.

In the mean time, Hannibal began to find himself reduced to great difficulty in obtaining provisions for his men. The policy of Fabius had been so far successful as to place him in a very embarrassing situation, and one growing more and more embarrassing every day. He could obtain no food except what he got by plunder, and there was now very little opportunity for that, as the inhabitants of the country had carried off all the grain and deposited it in strongly-fortified towns; and though Hannibal had great confidence in his power to cope with the Roman army in a regular battle on an open field, he had not strength sufficient to reduce citadels or attack fortified camps. His stock of provisions had become, therefore, more and more nearly exhausted, until now he had a supply for only ten days, and he saw no possible mode of increasing it.

His great object was, therefore, to bring on a battle. Varro was ready and willing to give him battle, but Æmilius, or, to call him by his name in full, Paulus Æmilius, which is the appellation by which he is more frequently known, was very desirous to persevere in the Fabian policy till the ten days had expired, after which he knew that Hannibal must be reduced to extreme distress, and might have to surrender at once to save his army from actual famine. In fact, it was said that the troops were on such short allowance as to produce great discontent, and that a large body of Spaniards were preparing to desert and go over together to the Roman camp.

Things were in this state, when, one day, Hannibal sent out a party from his camp to procure food, and Æmilius, who happened to hold the command that day, sent out a strong force to intercept them. He was successful. The Carthaginian detachment was routed. Nearly two thousand men were killed, and the rest fled, by any roads they could find, back to Hannibal's camp. Varro was very eager to follow them there, but Æmilius ordered his men to halt. He was afraid of some trick or treachery on the part of Hannibal, and was disposed to be satisfied with the victory he had already won.

This little success, however, only inflamed Varro's ardor for a battle, and produced a general enthusiasm in the Roman army; and, a day or two afterward, a circumstance occurred which raised this excitement to the highest pitch. Some reconnoiterers, who had been stationed within sight of Hannibal's camp to watch the motions and indications there, sent in word to the consuls that the Carthaginian guards around their encampment had all suddenly disappeared, and that a very extraordinary and unusual silence reigned within. Parties of the Roman soldiers went up gradually and cautiously to the Carthaginian lines, and soon found that the camp was deserted, though the fires were still burning and the tents remained. This intelligence, of course, put the whole Roman army into a fever of excitement and agitation. They crowded around the consuls' pavilions, and clamorously insisted on being led on to take possession of the camp, and to pursue the enemy. "He has fled," they said, "and with such precipitation that he has left the tents standing and his fires still burning. Lead us on in pursuit of him."

Varro was as much excited as the rest. He was eager for action. Æmilius hesitated. He made particular inquiries. He said they ought to proceed with caution. Finally, he called up a certain prudent and sagacious officer, named Statilius, and ordered him to take a small body of horsemen, ride over to the Carthaginian camp, ascertain the facts exactly, and report the result. Statilius did so. When he reached the lines he ordered his troops to halt, and took with him two horsemen on whose courage and strength he could rely, and rode in. The three horsemen rode around the camp and examined every thing with a view of ascertaining whether Hannibal had really abandoned his position and fled, or whether some stratagem was intended.

When he came back he reported to the army that, in his opinion, the desertion of the camp was not real, but a trick to draw the Romans into some difficulty. The fires were the largest on the side toward the Romans, which indicated that they were built to deceive. He saw money, too, and other valuables strewed about upon the ground, which appeared to him much more like a bait set in a trap, than like property abandoned by fugitives as incumbrances to flight. Varro was not convinced; and the army, hearing of the money, were excited to a greater eagerness for plunder. They could hardly be restrained. Just then, however, two slaves that had been taken prisoners by the Carthaginians some time before, came into the Roman camp. They told the consuls that the whole Carthaginian force was hid in ambush very near, waiting for the Romans to enter their encampment, when they were going to surround them and cut them to pieces. In the bustle and movement attendant on this plan, the slaves had escaped. Of course, the Roman army were now satisfied. They returned, chagrined and disappointed, to their own quarters, and Hannibal, still more chagrined and disappointed, returned to his.

He soon found, however, that he could not remain any longer where he was. His provisions were exhausted, and he could obtain no more. The Romans would not come out of their encampment to give him battle on equal terms, and they were too strongly intrenched to be attacked where they were. He determined, therefore, to evacuate that part of the country, and move, by a sudden march, into Apulia.

Apulia was on the eastern side of Italy. The River Aufidus runs through it, having a town named Cannæ near its mouth. The region of the Aufidus was a warm and sunny valley, which was now waving with ripening grain. Being further south than the place where he had been, and more exposed to the influence of the sun, Hannibal thought that the crops would be sooner ripe, and that, at least, he should have a new field to plunder.

He accordingly decided now to leave his camp in earnest, and move into Apulia. He made the same arrangements as before, when his departure was a mere pretense. He left tents pitched and fires burning, but marched his army off the ground by night and secretly, so that the Romans did not perceive his departure; and the next day, when they saw the appearances of silence and solitude about the camp, they suspected another deception, and made no move themselves. At length, however, intelligence came that the long columns of Hannibal's army had been seen already far to the eastward, and moving on as fast as possible, with all their baggage. The Romans, after much debate and uncertainty, resolved to follow. The eagles of the Apennines looked down upon the two great moving masses, creeping slowly along through the forests and valleys, like swarms of insects, one following the other, led on by a strange but strong attraction, drawing them toward each other when at a distance, but kept asunder by a still stronger repulsion when near.

The Roman army came up with that of Hannibal on the River Aufidus, near Cannæ, and the two vast encampments were formed with all the noise and excitement attendant on the movements of two great armies posting themselves on the eve of a battle, in the neighborhood of each other. In the Roman camp, the confusion was greatly aggravated by the angry disputes which immediately arose between the consuls and their respective adherents as to the course to be pursued. Varro insisted on giving the Carthaginians immediate battle. Æmilius refused. Varro said that he must protest against continuing any longer these inexcusable delays, and insist on a battle. He could not consent to be responsible any further for allowing Italy to lie at the mercy of such a scourge. Æmilius replied, that if Varro did precipitate a battle, he himself protested against his rashness, and could not be, in any degree, responsible for the result. The various officers took sides, some with one consul and some with the other, but most with Varro. The dissension filled the camp with excitement, agitation, and ill will.

In the mean time, the inhabitants of the country into which these two vast hordes of ferocious, though restrained and organized combatants, had made such a sudden irruption, were flying as fast as they could from the awful scene which they expected was to ensue. They carried from their villages and cabins what little property could be saved, and took the women and children away to retreats and fastnesses, wherever they imagined they could find temporary concealment or protection. The news of the movement of the two armies spread throughout the country, carried by hundreds of refugees and messengers, and all Italy, looking on with suspense and anxiety, awaited the result.

The armies maneuvered for a day or two, Varro, during his term of command, making arrangements to promote and favor an action, and Æmilius, on the following day, doing every thing in his power to prevent it. In the end, Varro succeeded. The lines were formed and the battle must be begun. Æmilius gave up the contest now, and while he protested earnestly against the course which Varro pursued, he prepared to do all in his power to prevent a defeat, since there was no longer a possibility of avoiding a collision.

The battle began, and the reader must imagine the scene, since no pen can describe it. Fifty thousand men on one side and eighty thousand on the other, at work hard and steadily, for six hours, killing each other by every possible means of destruction—stabs, blows, struggles, outcries, shouts of anger and defiance, and screams of terror and agony, all mingled together, in one general din, which covered the whole country for an extent of many miles, all together constituted a scene of horror of which none but those who have witnessed great battles can form any adequate idea.

It seems as if Hannibal could do nothing without stratagem. In the early part of this conflict he sent a large body of his troops over to the Romans as deserters. They threw down their spears and bucklers, as they reached the Roman lines, in token of surrender. The Romans received them, opened a passage for them through into the rear, and ordered them to remain there. As they were apparently unarmed, they left only a very small guard to keep them in custody. The men had, however, daggers concealed about their dress, and, watching a favorable moment, in the midst of the battle, they sprang to their feet, drew out their weapons, broke away from their guard, and attacked the Romans in the rear at a moment when they were so pressed by the enemy in front that they could scarcely maintain their ground.

It was evident before many hours that the Roman forces were every where yielding. From slowly and reluctantly yielding they soon began to fly. In the flight, the weak and the wounded were trampled under foot by the throng who were pressing on behind them, or were dispatched by wanton blows from enemies as they passed in pursuit of those who were still able to fly. In the midst of this scene, a Roman officer named Lentulus, as he was riding away, saw before him at the road-side another officer wounded, sitting upon a stone, faint and bleeding. He stopped when he reached him, and found that it was the consul Æmilius. He had been wounded in the head with a sling, and his strength was almost gone. Lentulus offered him his horse, and urged him to take it and fly. Æmilius declined the offer. He said it was too late for his life to be saved, and that, besides, he had no wish to save it. "Go on, therefore, yourself," said he, "as fast as you can. Make the best of your way to Rome. Tell the authorities there, from me, that all is lost, and they must do whatever they can themselves for the defense of the city. Make all the speed you can, or Hannibal will be at the gates before you."

Æmilius sent also a message to Fabius, declaring to him that it was not his fault that a battle had been risked with Hannibal. He had done all in his power, he said, to prevent it, and had adhered to the policy which Fabius had recommended to the last. Lentulus having received these messages, and perceiving that the Carthaginians were close upon him in pursuit, rode away, leaving the consul to his fate. The Carthaginians came on, and, on seeing the wounded man, they thrust their spears into his body, one after another, as they passed, until his limbs ceased to quiver. As for the other consul, Varro, he escaped with his life. Attended by about seventy horsemen, he made his way to a fortified town not very remote from the battle-field, where he halted with his horsemen, and determined that he would attempt to rally there the remains of the army.

The Carthaginians, when they found the victory complete, abandoned the pursuit of the enemy, returned to their camp, spent some hours in feasting and rejoicing, and then laid down to sleep. They were, of course, well exhausted by the intense exertions of the day. On the field where the battle had been fought, the wounded lay all night mingled with the dead, filling the air with cries and groans, and writhing in their agony.

Early the next morning the Carthaginians came back to the field to plunder the dead bodies of the Romans. The whole field presented a most shocking spectacle to the view. The bodies of horses and men lay mingled in dreadful confusion, as they had fallen, some dead, others still alive, the men moaning, crying for water, and feebly struggling from time to time to disentangle themselves from the heaps of carcasses under which they were buried. The deadly and inextinguishable hate which the Carthaginians felt for their foes not having been appeased by the slaughter of forty thousand of them, they beat down and stabbed these wretched lingerers wherever they found them, as a sort of morning pastime after the severer labors of the preceding day. This slaughter, however, could hardly be considered a cruelty to the wretched victims of it, for many of them bared their breasts to their assailants, and begged for the blow which was to put an end to their pain. In exploring the field, one Carthaginian soldier was found still alive, but imprisoned by the dead body of his Roman enemy lying upon him. The Carthaginian's face and ears were shockingly mangled. The Roman, having fallen upon him when both were mortally wounded, had continued the combat with his teeth when he could no longer use his weapon, and had died at last, binding down his exhausted enemy with his own dead body.

The Carthaginians secured a vast amount of plunder. The Roman army was full of officers and soldiers from the aristocratic ranks of society, and their arms and their dress were very valuable. The Carthaginians obtained some bushels of gold rings from their fingers, which Hannibal sent to Carthage as a trophy of his victory.

10

Scipio

THE true reason why Hannibal could not be arrested in his triumphant career seems not to have been because the Romans did not pursue the right kind of policy toward him, but because, thus far, they had no general who was his equal. Whoever was sent against him soon proved to be his inferior. Hannibal could out-maneuver them all in stratagem, and could conquer them on the field. There was, however, now destined to appear a man capable of coping with Hannibal. It was young Scipio, the one who saved the life of his father at the battle of Ticinus. This Scipio, though the son of Hannibal's first great antagonist of that name, is commonly called, in history, the elder Scipio; for there was another of his name after him, who was greatly celebrated for his wars against the Carthaginians in Africa. These last two received from the Roman people the surname of Africanus, in honor of their African victories, and the one who now comes upon the stage was called Scipio Africanus the elder, or sometimes simply the elder Scipio. The deeds of the Scipio who attempted to stop Hannibal at the Rhone and upon the Po were so wholly eclipsed by his son, and by the other Scipio who followed him, that the former is left out of view and forgotten in designating and distinguishing the others.

Our present Scipio first appears upon the stage, in the exercise of military command, after the battle of Cannæ. He was a subordinate officer and on the day following the battle he found himself at a place called Canusium, which was at a short distance from Cannæ, on the way toward Rome, with a number of other officers of his own rank, and with broken masses and detachments of the army coming in from time to time, faint, exhausted, and in despair. The rumor was that both consuls were killed. These fragments of the army had, therefore, no one to command them. The officers met together, and unanimously agreed to make Scipio their commander in the emergency, until some superior officer should arrive, or they should get orders from Rome.

An incident here occurred which showed, in a striking point of view, the boldness and energy of the young Scipio's character. At the very meeting in which he was placed in command, and when they were overwhelmed with perplexity and care, an officer came in, and reported that in another part of the camp there was an assembly of officers and young men of rank, headed by a certain Metellus, who had decided to give up the cause of their country in despair, and that they were making arrangements to proceed immediately to the sea-coast, obtain ships, and sail away to seek a new home in some foreign lands, considering their cause in Italy as utterly lost and ruined. The officer proposed that they should call a council and deliberate what was best to do.

"Deliberate!" said Scipio; "this is not a case for deliberation, but for action. Draw your swords and follow me." So saying, he pressed forward at the head of the party to the quarters of Metellus. They marched boldly into the apartment where he and his friends were in consultation. Scipio held up his sword, and in a very solemn manner pronounced an oath, binding himself not to abandon his country in this the hour of her distress, nor to allow any other Roman citizen to abandon her. If he should be guilty of such treason, he called upon Jupiter, by the most dreadful imprecations, to destroy him utterly, house, family, fortune, soul, and body.

"And now, Metellus, I call upon you," said he, "and all who are with you, to take the same oath. You must do it, otherwise you have got to defend yourselves against these swords of ours, as well as those of the Carthaginians." Metellus and his party yielded. Nor was it wholly to fear that they yielded. It was to the influence of hope quite as much as to that of fear. The courage, the energy, and the martial ardor which Scipio's conduct evinced, awakened a similar spirit in them, and made them hope again that possibly their country might yet be saved.

The news of the awful defeat and destruction of the Roman army flew swiftly to Rome, and produced universal consternation. The whole city was in an uproar. There were soldiers in the army from almost every family, so that every woman and child throughout the city was distracted by the double agitation of inconsolable grief at the death of their husband or their father, slain in the battle, and of terrible fear that Hannibal and his raging followers were about to burst in through the gates of the city to murder them. The streets of the city, and especially the Forum, were thronged with vast crowds of men, women, and children, who filled the air with loud lamentations, and with cries of terror and despair.

The magistrates were not able to restore order. The senate actually adjourned, that the members of it might go about the city, and use their influence and their power to produce silence at least, if they could not restore composure. The streets were finally cleared. The women and children were ordered to remain at home. Armed patrols were put on guard to prevent tumultuous assemblies forming. Men were sent off on horseback on the road to Canusium and Cannæ, to get more accurate intelligence, and then the senate assembled again, and began to consider, with as much of calmness as they could command, what was to be done.

The panic at Rome was, however, in some measure, a false alarm, for Hannibal, contrary to the expectation of all Italy, did not go to Rome. His generals urged him very strongly to do so. Nothing could prevent, they said, his gaining immediate possession of the city. But Hannibal refused to do this. Rome was strongly fortified, and had an immense population. His army, too, was much weakened by the battle of Cannæ, and he seems to have thought it most prudent not to attempt the reduction of Rome until he should have received re-enforcements from home. It was now so late in the season that he could not expect such re-enforcements immediately, and he accordingly determined to select some place more accessible than Rome, and make it his head-quarters for the winter. He decided in favor of Capua, which was a large and powerful city one or two hundred miles southeast of Rome.

Hannibal, in fact, conceived the design of retaining possession of Italy and of making Capua the capital of the country, leaving Rome to itself, to decline, as under such circumstances it inevitably must, to the rank of a second city. Perhaps he was tired of the fatigues and hazards of war, and having narrowly escaped ruin before the battle of Cannæ, he now resolved that he would not rashly incur any new dangers. It was a great question with him whether he should go forward to Rome, or attempt to build up a new capital of his own at Capua. The question which of these two he ought to have done was a matter of great debate then, and it has been discussed a great deal by military men in every age since his day. Right or wrong, Hannibal decided to establish his own capital at Capua, and to leave Rome, for the present, undisturbed.

He, however, sent immediately to Carthage for re-enforcements. The messenger whom he sent was one of his generals named Mago. Mago made the best of his way to Carthage with his tidings of victory and his bushel of rings, collected, as has been already said, from the field of Cannæ. The city of Carthage was greatly excited by the news which he brought. The friends and patrons of Hannibal were elated with enthusiasm and pride, and they taunted and reproached his enemies with the opposition to him they had manifested when he was originally appointed to the command of the army of Spain.

Mago met the Carthaginian senate, and in a very spirited and eloquent speech he told them how many glorious battles Hannibal had fought, and how many victories he had won. He had contended with the greatest generals that the Romans could bring against him, and had conquered them all. He had slain, he said, in all, over two hundred thousand men. All Italy was now subject to his power; Capua was his capital, and Rome had fallen. He concluded by saying that Hannibal was in need of considerable additional supplies of men, and money, and provisions, which he did not doubt the Carthaginians would send without any unnecessary delay. He then produced before the senate the great bag of rings which he had brought, and poured them upon the pavement of the senate-house as a trophy of the victories which he had been announcing.

This would, perhaps, have all been very well for Hannibal if his friends had been contented to have left the case where Mago left it; but some of them could not resist the temptation of taunting his enemies, and especially Hanno, who, as will be recollected, originally opposed his being sent to Spain. They turned to him, and asked him triumphantly what he thought now of his factious opposition to so brave a warrior. Hanno rose. The senate looked toward him and were profoundly silent, wondering what he would have to reply. Hanno, with an air of perfect ease and composure, spoke somewhat as follows:

"I should have said nothing, but should have allowed the senate to take what action they pleased on Mago's proposition if I had not been particularly addressed. As it is, I will say that I think now just as I always have thought. We are plunged into a most costly and most useless war, and are, as I conceive, no nearer the end of it now than ever, notwithstanding all these boasted successes. The emptiness of them is clearly shown by the inconsistency of Hannibal's pretensions as to what he has done, with the demands that he makes in respect to what he wishes us to do. He says he has conquered all his enemies, and yet he wants us to send him more soldiers. He has reduced all Italy—the most fertile country in the world—to subjection, and reigns over it at Capua, and yet he calls upon us for corn. And then, to crown all, he sends us bushels of gold rings as a specimen of the riches he has obtained by plunder, and accompanies the offering with a demand for new supplies of money. In my opinion, his success is all illusive and hollow. There seems to be nothing substantial in his situation except his necessities, and the heavy burdens upon the state which these necessities impose."

Notwithstanding Hanno's sarcasms, the Carthaginians resolved to sustain Hannibal, and to send him the supplies that he needed. They were, however, long in reaching him. Various difficulties and delays occurred. The Romans, though they could not dispossess Hannibal from his position in Italy, raised armies in different countries, and waged extended wars with the Carthaginians and their allies, in various parts of the world, both by sea and land.

The result was, that Hannibal remained fifteen or sixteen years in Italy, engaged, during all this time, in a lingering struggle with the Roman power, without ever being able to accomplish any decisive measures. During this period he was sometimes successful and victorious, and sometimes he was very hard pressed by his enemies. It is said that his army was very much enervated and enfeebled by the comforts and luxuries they enjoyed at Capua. Capua was a very rich and beautiful city, and the inhabitants of it had opened their gates to Hannibal of their own accord, preferring, as they said, his alliance to that of the Romans. The officers—as the officers of an army almost always do, when they find themselves established in a rich and powerful city, after the fatigues of a long and honorable campaign—gave themselves up to festivities and rejoicing, to games, shows, and entertainments of every kind, which they soon learned infinitely to prefer to the toil and danger of marches and battles.

Whatever may have been the cause, there is no question about the fact that, from the time Hannibal and his army got possession of their comfortable quarters in Capua, the Carthaginian power began gradually to decline. As Hannibal determined to make that city the Italian capital instead of Rome, he, of course, when established there, felt in some degree settled and at home, and was less interested than he had been in plans for attacking the ancient capital. Still, the war went on; many battles were fought, many cities were besieged, the Roman power gaining ground all the time, though not, however, by any very decisive victories.

In these contests there appeared, at length, a new Roman general named Marcellus, and, either on account of his possessing a bolder and more active temperament, or else in consequence of the change in the relative strength of the two contending powers, he pursued a more aggressive policy than Fabius had thought it prudent to attempt. Marcellus was, however, cautious and wary in his enterprises, and he laid his plans with so much sagacity and skill that he was almost always successful. The Romans applauded very highly his activity and ardor, without, however, forgetting their obligations to Fabius for his caution and defensive reserve. They said that Marcellus was the sword of their commonwealth, as Fabius had been its shield.

The Romans continued to prosecute this sort of warfare, being more and more successful the longer they continued it, until, at last, they advanced to the very walls of Capua, and threatened it with a siege. Hannibal's intrenchments and fortifications were too strong for them to attempt to carry the city by a sudden assault, nor were the Romans even powerful enough to invest the place entirely, so as completely to shut their enemies in. They, however, encamped with a large army in the neighborhood, and assumed so threatening an attitude as to keep Hannibal's forces within in a state of continual alarm. And, besides the alarm, it was very humiliating and mortifying to Carthaginian pride to find the very seat of their power, as it were, shut up and overawed by an enemy over whom they had been triumphing themselves so short a time before, by a continued series of victories.

Hannibal was not himself in Capua at the time that the Romans came to attack it. He marched, however, immediately to its relief, and, attacking the Romans in his turn, endeavored to compel them to raise the siege, as it is technically termed, and retire. They had, however, so intrenched themselves in the positions that they had taken, and the assaults with which he encountered them had lost so much of their former force, that he could accomplish nothing decisive. He then left the ground with his army, and marched himself toward Rome. He encamped in the vicinity of the city, and threatened to attack it; but the walls, and castles, and towers with which Rome, as well as Capua, was defended, were too formidable, and the preparations for defense too complete, to make it prudent for him really to assail the city. His object was to alarm the Romans, and compel them to withdraw their forces from his capital that they might defend their own.

There was, in fact, some degree of alarm awakened, and in the discussions which took place among the Roman authorities, the withdrawal of their troops from Capua was proposed; but this proposal was overruled; even Fabius was against it. Hannibal was no longer to be feared. They ordered back a small detachment from Capua, and added to it such forces as they could raise within the city, and then advanced to give Hannibal battle. The preparations were all made, it is said, for an engagement, but a violent storm came on, so violent as to drive the combatants back to their respective camps. This happened, the great Roman historian gravely says, two or three times in succession; the weather immediately becoming serene again, each time, as soon as the respective generals had withdrawn their troops from the intended fight. Something like this may perhaps have occurred, though the fact doubtless was that both parties were afraid, each of the other, and were disposed to avail themselves of any excuse to postpone a decisive conflict. There was a time when Hannibal had not been deterred from attacking the Romans even by the most tempestuous storms.

Thus, though Hannibal did, in fact, in the end, get to the walls of Rome, he did nothing but threaten when he was there, and his encampment near the city can only be considered as a bravado. His presence seems to have excited very little apprehension within the city. The Romans had, in fact, before this time, lost their terror of the Carthaginian arms. To show their contempt of Hannibal, they sold, at public auction, the land on which he was encamped, while he was upon it besieging the city, and it brought the usual price. The bidders were, perhaps, influenced somewhat by a patriotic spirit, and by a desire to taunt Hannibal with an expression of their opinion that his occupation of the land would be a very temporary encumbrance. Hannibal, to revenge himself for this taunt, put up for sale at auction, in his own camp, the shops of one of the principal streets of Rome, and they were bought by his officers with great spirit. It showed that a great change had taken place in the nature of the contest between Carthage and Rome, to find these vast powers, which were a few years before grappling each other with such destructive and terrible fury on the Po and at Cannæ, now satisfying their declining animosity with such squibbing as this.

When the other modes by which Hannibal attempted to obtain re-enforcements failed, he made an attempt to have a second army brought over the Alps under the command of his brother Hasdrubal. It was a large army, and in their march they experienced the same difficulties, though in a much lighter degree, that Hannibal had himself encountered. And yet, of the whole mighty mass which set out from Spain, nothing reached Hannibal except his brother's head. The circumstances of the unfortunate termination of Hasdrubal's attempt were as follows:

When Hasdrubal descended from the Alps, rejoicing in the successful manner in which he had surmounted those formidable barriers, he imagined that all his difficulties were over. He dispatched couriers to his brother Hannibal, informing him that he had scaled the mountains, and that he was coming on as rapidly as possible to his aid.

The two consuls in office at this time were named, the one Nero, and the other Livius. To each of these, as was usual with the Roman consuls, was assigned a particular province, and a certain portion of the army to defend it, and the laws enjoined it upon them very strictly not to leave their respective provinces, on any pretext whatever, without authority from the Roman Legislature. In this instance Livius had been assigned to the northern part of Italy, and Nero to the southern. It devolved upon Livius, therefore, to meet and give battle to Hasdrubal on his descent from the Alps, and to Nero to remain in the vicinity of Hannibal, to thwart his plans, oppose his progress, and, if possible, conquer and destroy him, while his colleague prevented his receiving the expected re-enforcements from Spain.

Things being in this state, the couriers whom Hasdrubal sent with his letters had the vigilance of both consuls to elude before they could deliver them into Hannibal's hands. They did succeed in passing Livius, but they were intercepted by Nero. The patrols who seized these messengers brought them to Nero's tent. Nero opened and read the letters. All Hasdrubal's plans and arrangements were detailed in them very fully, so that Nero perceived that, if he were at once to proceed to the northward with a strong force, he could render his colleague such aid as, with the knowledge of Hasdrubal's plans, which he had obtained from the letters, would probably enable them to defeat him; whereas, if he were to leave Livius in ignorance and alone, he feared that Hasdrubal would be successful in breaking his way through, and in ultimately effecting his junction with Hannibal. Under these circumstances, he was, of course, very earnestly desirous of going northward to render the necessary aid, but he was strictly forbidden by law to leave his own province to enter that of his colleague without an authority from Rome, which there was not now time to obtain.

The laws of military discipline are very strict and imperious, and in theory they are never to be disobeyed. Officers and soldiers, of all ranks and gradations, must obey the orders which they receive from the authority above them, without looking at the consequences, or deviating from the line marked out on any pretext whatever. It is, in fact, the very essence of military subordination and efficiency, that a command, once given, suspends all exercise of judgment or discretion on the part of the one to whom it is addressed; and a good general or a good government would prefer generally that harm should be done by a strict obedience to commands, rather than a benefit secured by an unauthorized deviation from them. It is a good principle, not only in war, but in all those cases in social life where men have to act in concert, and yet wish to secure efficiency in action.

And yet there are cases of exception—cases where the necessity is so urgent, or the advantages to be derived are so great; where the interests involved are so momentous, and the success so sure, that a commander concludes to disobey and take the responsibility. The responsibility is, however, very great, and the danger in assuming it extreme. He who incurs it makes himself liable to the severest penalties, from which nothing but clear proof of the most imperious necessity, and, in addition to it, the most triumphant success, can save him. There is somewhere in English history a story of a naval commander, in the service of an English queen, who disobeyed the orders of his superiors at one time, in a case of great emergency at sea, and gained by so doing a very important victory. Immediately afterward he placed himself under arrest, and went into port as a prisoner accused of crime instead of a commander triumphing in his victory. He surrendered himself to the queen's officers of justice, and sent word to the queen herself that he knew very well that death was the penalty for his offense, but that he was willing to sacrifice his life in any way in the service of her majesty. He was pardoned!

Nero, after much anxious deliberation, concluded that the emergency in which he found himself placed was one requiring him to take the responsibility of disobedience. He did not, however, dare to go northward with all his forces, for that would be to leave southern Italy wholly at the mercy of Hannibal. He selected, therefore, from his whole force, which consisted of forty thousand men, seven or eight thousand of the most efficient and trustworthy; the men on whom he could most securely rely, both in respect to their ability to bear the fatigues of a rapid march, and the courage and energy with which they would meet Hasdrubal's forces in battle at the end of it. He was, at the time when Hasdrubal's letters were intercepted, occupying a spacious and well-situated camp. This he enlarged and strengthened, so that Hannibal might not suspect that he intended any diminution of the forces within. All this was done very promptly, so that, in a few hours after he received the intelligence on which he was acting, he was drawing off secretly, at night, a column of six or eight thousand men, none of whom knew at all where they were going.

He proceeded as rapidly as possible to the northward, and, when he arrived in the northern province, he contrived to get into the camp of Livius as secretly as he had got out from his own. Thus, of the two armies, the one where an accession of force was required was greatly strengthened at the expense of the other, without either of the Carthaginian generals having suspected the change.

Livius was rejoiced to get so opportune a re-enforcement. He recommended that the troops should all remain quietly in camp for a short time, until the newly-arrived troops could rest and recruit themselves a little after their rapid and fatiguing march; but Nero opposed this plan, and recommended an immediate battle. He knew the character of the men that he had brought, and he was, besides, unwilling to risk the dangers which might arise in his own camp, in southern Italy, by too long an absence from it. It was decided, accordingly, to attack Hasdrubal at once, and the signal for battle was given.

It is not improbable that Hasdrubal would have been beaten by Livius alone, but the additional force which Nero had brought made the Romans altogether too strong for him. Besides, from his position in the front of the battle, he perceived, from some indications that his watchful eye observed, that a part of the troops attacking him were from the southward; and he inferred from this that Hannibal had been defeated, and that, in consequence of this, the whole united force of the Roman army was arrayed against him. He was disheartened and discouraged, and soon ordered a retreat. He was pursued by the various divisions of the Roman army, and the retreating columns of the Carthaginians were soon thrown into complete confusion. They became entangled among rivers and lakes; and the guides who had undertaken to conduct the army; finding that all was lost, abandoned them and fled, anxious only to save their own lives. The Carthaginians were soon pent up in a position where they could not defend themselves, and from which they could not escape. The Romans showed them no mercy, but went on killing their wretched and despairing victims until the whole army was almost totally destroyed. They cut off Hasdrubal's head, and Nero set out the very night after the battle to return with it in triumph to his own encampment. When he arrived, he sent a troop of horse to throw the head over into Hannibal's camp, a ghastly and horrid trophy of his victory.

Hasdrubal's Head.

Hannibal was overwhelmed with disappointment and sorrow at the loss of his army, bringing with it, as it did, the destruction of all his hopes. "My fate is sealed," said he: "all is lost. I shall send no more news of victory to Carthage. In losing Hasdrubal my last hope is gone."

While Hannibal was in this condition in Italy, the Roman armies, aided by their allies, were gaining gradually against the Carthaginians in various parts of the world, under the different generals who had been placed in command by the Roman senate. The news of these victories came continually home to Italy, and encouraged and animated the Romans, while Hannibal and his army, as well as the people who were in alliance with him, were disheartened and depressed by them. Scipio was one of these generals commanding in foreign lands. His province was Spain. The news which came home from his army became more and more exciting, as he advanced from conquest to conquest, until it seemed that the whole country was going to be reduced to subjection. He overcame one Carthaginian general after another until he reached

New Carthage, which he besieged and conquered, and the Roman authority was established fully over the whole land.

Scipio then returned in triumph to Rome. The people received him with acclamations. At the next election they chose him consul. On the allotment of provinces, Sicily fell to him, with power to cross into Africa if he pleased. It devolved on the other consul to carry on the war in Italy more directly against Hannibal. Scipio levied his army, equipped his fleet, and sailed for Sicily.

The first thing that he did on his arrival in his province was to project an expedition into Africa itself. He could not, as he wished, face Hannibal directly, by marching his troops into the south of Italy, for this was the work allotted to his colleague. He could, however, make an incursion into Africa, and even threaten Carthage itself, and this, with the boldness and ardor which marked his character, he resolved to do.

He was triumphantly successful in all his plans. His army, imbibing the spirit of enthusiasm which animated their commander, and confident of success, went on, as his forces in Spain had done, from victory to victory. They conquered cities, they overran provinces, they defeated and drove back all the armies which the Carthaginians could bring against them, and finally they awakened in the streets and dwellings of Carthage the same panic and consternation which Hannibal's victorious progress had produced in Rome.

The Carthaginians being now, in their turn, reduced to despair, sent embassadors to Scipio to beg for peace, and to ask on what terms he would grant it and withdraw from the country. Scipio replied that he could not make peace. It rested with the Roman senate, whose servant he was. He specified, however, certain terms which he was willing to have proposed to the senate, and, if the Carthaginians would agree to them, he would grant them a truce, that is, a temporary suspension of hostilities, until the answer of the Roman senate could be returned.

The Carthaginians agreed to the terms. They were very onerous. The Romans say that they did not really mean to abide by them, but acceded for the moment in order to gain time to send for Hannibal. They had great confidence in his resources and military power, and thought that, if he were in Africa, he could save them. At the same time, therefore, that they sent their embassadors to Rome with their propositions for peace, they dispatched expresses to Hannibal, ordering him to embark his troops as soon as possible, and, abandoning Italy, to hasten home, to save, if it was not already too late, his native city from destruction.

When Hannibal received these messages, he was overwhelmed with disappointment and sorrow. He spent hours in extreme agitation, sometimes in a moody silence, interrupted now and then by groans of despair, and sometimes uttering loud and angry curses, prompted by the exasperation of his feelings. He, however, could not resist. He made the best of his way to Carthage. The Roman senate, at the same time, instead of deciding on the question of peace or war, which Scipio had submitted to them, referred the question back to him. They sent commissioners to Scipio, authorizing him to act for them, and to decide himself alone whether the war should be continued or closed, and if to be closed, on what conditions.

Hannibal raised a large force at Carthage, joining with it such remains of former armies as had been left after Scipio's battles, and he went forth at the head of these troops to meet his enemy. He marched five days, going, perhaps, seventy-five or one hundred miles from Carthage, when he found himself approaching Scipio's camp. He sent out spies to reconnoiter. The patrols of Scipio's army seized these spies, and brought them to the general's tent, as they supposed, for execution. Instead of punishing them, Scipio ordered them to be led around his camp, and to be allowed to see every thing they desired. He then dismissed them that they might return to Hannibal with the information they had obtained.

Of course, the report which they brought in respect to the strength and resources of Scipio's army was very formidable to Hannibal. He thought it best to make an attempt to negotiate a peace rather than to risk a battle, and he accordingly sent word to Scipio requesting a personal interview. Scipio acceded to this request, and a place was appointed for the meeting between the two encampments. To this spot the two generals repaired at the proper time, with great pomp and parade, and with many attendants. They were the two greatest generals of the age in which they lived, having been engaged for fifteen or twenty years in performing, at the head of vast armies, exploits which had filled the world with their fame. Their fields of action had, however, been widely distant, and they met personally now for the first time. When introduced into each other's presence, they stood for some time in silence, gazing upon and examining one another with intense interest and curiosity, but not speaking a word.

At length, however, the negotiation was opened. Hannibal made Scipio proposals for peace. They were very favorable to the Romans, but Scipio was not satisfied with them, He demanded still greater sacrifices than Hannibal was willing to make. The result, after a long and fruitless negotiation, was, that each general returned to his camp and prepared for battle.

In military campaigns, it is generally easy for those who have been conquering to go on to conquer: so much depends upon the expectations with which the contending armies go into battle. Scipio and his troops expected to conquer. The Carthaginians expected to be beaten. The result corresponded. At the close of the day on which the battle was fought, forty thousand Carthaginians were dead and dying upon the ground, as many more were prisoners in the Roman camp, and the rest, in broken masses, were flying from the field in confusion and terror, on all the roads which led to Carthage. Hannibal arrived at the city with the rest, went to the senate, announced his defeat, and said that he could do no more. "The fortune which once attended me," said he, "is lost forever, and nothing is left to us but to make peace with our enemies on any terms that they may think fit to impose."

11

Hannibal a Fugitive and an Exile

HANNIBAL'S life was like an April day. Its brightest glory was in the morning. The setting of his sun was darkened by clouds and showers. Although for fifteen years the Roman people could find no general capable of maintaining the field against him, Scipio conquered him at last, and all his brilliant conquests ended, as Hanno had predicted, only in placing his country in a far worse condition than before.

In fact, as long as the Carthaginians confined their energies to useful industry, and to the pursuits of commerce and peace, they were prosperous, and they increased in wealth, and influence, and honor every year. Their ships went every where, and were every where welcome. All the shores of the Mediterranean were visited by their merchants, and the comforts and the happiness of many nations and tribes were promoted by the very means which they took to swell their own riches and fame. All might have gone on so for centuries longer, had not military heroes arisen with appetites for a more piquant sort of glory. Hannibal's father was one of the foremost of these. He began by conquests in Spain and encroachments on the Roman jurisdiction. He inculcated the same feelings of ambition and hate in Hannibal's mind which burned in his own. For many years, the policy which they led their countrymen to pursue was successful. From being useful and welcome visitors to all the world, they became the masters and the curse of a part of it. So long as Hannibal remained superior to any Roman general that could be brought against him, he went on conquering. But at last Scipio arose, a greater than Hannibal. The tide was then turned, and all the vast conquests of half a century were wrested away by the same violence, bloodshed, and misery with which they had been acquired.

We have described the exploits of Hannibal, in making these conquests, in detail, while those of Scipio, in wresting them away, have been passed over very briefly, as this is intended as a history of Hannibal, and not of Scipio. Still, Scipio's conquests were made by slow degrees, and they consumed a long period of time. He was but about eighteen years of age at the battle of Cannæ, soon after which his campaigns began, and he was thirty when he was made consul, just before his going into Africa. He was thus fifteen or eighteen years in taking down the vast superstructure of power which Hannibal had raised, working in regions away from Hannibal and Carthage during all this time, as if leaving the great general and the great city for the last. He was, however, so successful in what he did, that when, at length, he advanced to the attack of Carthage, every thing else was gone. The Carthaginian power had become a mere hollow shell, empty and vain, which required only one great final blow to effect its absolute demolition. In fact, so far spent and gone were all the Carthaginian resources, that the great city had to summon the great general to its aid the moment it was threatened, and Scipio destroyed them both together.

And yet Scipio did not proceed so far as literally and actually to destroy them. He spared Hannibal's life, and he allowed the city to stand; but the terms and conditions of peace which he exacted were such as to put an absolute and perpetual end to Carthaginian dominion. By these conditions, the Carthaginian state was allowed to continue free and independent, and even to retain the government of such territories in Africa as they possessed before the war; but all their foreign possessions were taken away; and even in respect to Africa, their jurisdiction was limited and curtailed by very hard restrictions. Their whole navy was to be given to the Romans except ten small ships of three banks of oars, which Scipio thought the government would need for the purposes of civil administration: These they were allowed to retain. Scipio did not say what he should do with the remainder of the fleet: it was to be unconditionally surrendered to him. Their elephants of war were also to be all given up, and they were to be bound not to train any more. They were not to appear at all as a military power in any other quarter of the world but Africa, and they were not to make war in Africa except by previously making known the occasion for it to the Roman people, and obtaining their permission. They were also to pay to the Romans a very large annual tribute for fifty years.

There was great distress and perplexity in the Carthaginian councils while they were debating these cruel terms. Hannibal was in favor of accepting them. Others opposed. They thought it would be better still to continue the struggle, hopeless as it was, than to submit to terms so ignominious and fatal.

Hannibal was present at these debates, but he found himself now in a very different position from that which he had been occupying for thirty years as a victorious general at the head of his army. He had been accustomed there to control and direct every thing. In his councils of war, no one spoke but at his invitation, and no opinion was expressed but such as he was willing to hear. In the Carthaginian senate, however, he found the case very different. There, opinions were freely expressed, as in a debate among equals, Hannibal taking his place among the rest, and counting only as one. And yet the spirit of authority and command which he had been so long accustomed to exercise, lingered still, and made him very impatient and uneasy under contradiction. In fact, as one of the speakers in the senate was rising to animadvert upon and oppose Hannibal's views, he undertook to pull him down and silence him by force. This proceeding awakened immediately such expressions of dissatisfaction and displeasure in the assembly as to show him very clearly that the time for such domineering was gone. He had, however, the good sense to express the regret he soon felt at having so far forgotten the duties of his new position, and to make an ample apology.

The Carthaginians decided at length to accede to Scipio's terms of peace. The first instalment of the tribute was paid. The elephants and the ships were surrendered. After a few days, Scipio announced his determination not to take the ships away with him, but to destroy them there. Perhaps this was because he thought the ships would be of little value to the Romans, on account of the difficulty of manning them. Ships, of course, are useless without seamen, and many nations in modern times, who could easily build a navy, are debarred from doing it, because their population does not furnish sailors in sufficient numbers to man and navigate it. It was probably, in part, on this account that Scipio decided not to take the Carthaginian ships away, and perhaps he also wanted to show to Carthage and to the world that his object in taking possession of the national property of his foes was not to enrich his own country by plunder, but only to deprive ambitious soldiers of the power to compromise any longer the peace and happiness of mankind by expeditions for conquest and power. However this may be, Scipio determined to destroy the Carthaginian fleet, and not to convey it away.

The Burning of the Carthaginian Fleet.

On a given day, therefore, he ordered all the galleys to be got together in the bay opposite to the city of Carthage, and to be burned. These were five hundred of them, so that they constituted a large fleet, and covered a large expanse of the water. A vast concourse of people assembled upon the shores to witness the grand conflagration. The emotion which such a spectacle was of itself calculated to excite was greatly heightened by the deep but stifled feelings of resentment and hate which agitated every Carthaginian breast. The Romans, too, as they gazed upon the scene from their encampment on the shore, were agitated as well, though with different emotions. Their faces beamed with an expression of exultation and triumph as they saw the vast masses of flame and columns of smoke ascending from the sea, proclaiming the total and irretrievable ruin of Carthaginian pride and power.

Having thus fully accomplished his work, Scipio set sail for Rome. All Italy had been filled with the fame of his exploits in thus destroying the ascendancy of Hannibal. The city of Rome had now nothing more to fear from its great enemy. He was shut up, disarmed, and helpless, in his own native state, and the terror which his presence in Italy had inspired had passed forever away. The whole population of Rome, remembering the awful scenes of consternation and terror which the city had so often endured, regarded Scipio as a great deliverer. They were eager to receive and welcome him on his arrival. When the time came and he approached the city, vast throngs went out to meet him. The authorities formed civic processions to welcome him. They brought crowns, and garlands, and flowers, and hailed his approach with loud and prolonged acclamations of triumph and joy. They gave him the name of Africanus, in honor of his victories. This was a new honor—giving to a conqueror the name of the country that he had subdued; it was invented specially as Scipio's reward, the deliverer who had saved the empire from the greatest and most terrible danger by which it had ever been assailed.

Hannibal, though fallen, retained still in Carthage some portion of his former power. The glory of his past exploits still invested his character with a sort of halo, which made him an object of general regard, and he still had great and powerful friends. He was elevated to high office, and exerted himself to regulate and improve the internal affairs of the state. In these efforts he was not, however, very successful. The historians say that the objects which he aimed to accomplish were good, and that the measures for effecting them were, in themselves, judicious; but, accustomed as he was to the authoritative and arbitrary action of a military commander in camp, he found it hard to practice that caution and forbearance, and that deference for the opinion of others, which are so essential as means of influencing men in the management of the civil affairs of a commonwealth. He made a great many enemies, who did every thing in their power, by plots and intrigues, as well as by open hostility, to accomplish his ruin.

His pride, too, was extremely mortified and humbled by an occurrence which took place very soon after Scipio's return to Rome. There was some occasion of war with a neighboring African tribe, and Hannibal headed some forces which were raised in the city for the purpose, and went out to prosecute it. The Romans who took care to have agents in Carthage to keep them acquainted with all that occurred, heard of this, and sent word to Carthage to warn the Carthaginians that this was contrary to the treaty, and could not be allowed. The government, not willing to incur the risk of another visit from Scipio, sent orders to Hannibal to abandon the war and return to the city. Hannibal was compelled to submit; but after having been accustomed, as he had been, for many years, to bid defiance to all the armies and fleets which Roman power could, with their utmost exertion, bring against him, it must have been very hard for such a spirit as his to find itself stopped and conquered now by a word. All the force they could command against him, even at the very gates of their own city, was once impotent and vain. Now, a mere message and threat, coming across the distant sea, seeks him out in the remote deserts of Africa, and in a moment deprives him of all his power.

Years passed away, and Hannibal, though compelled outwardly to submit to his fate, was restless and ill at ease. His scheming spirit, spurred on now by the double stimulus of resentment and ambition, was always busy, vainly endeavoring to discover some plan by which he might again renew the struggle with his ancient foe.

It will be recollected that Carthage was originally a commercial colony from Tyre, a city on the eastern shores of the Mediterranean Sea. The countries of Syria and Phœnicia were in the vicinity of Tyre. They were powerful commercial communities, and they had always retained very friendly relations with the Carthaginian commonwealth. Ships passed continually to and fro, and always, in case of calamities or disasters threatening one of these regions, the inhabitants naturally looked to the other for refuge and protection, Carthage looking upon Phœnicia as its mother, and Phœnicia regarding Carthage as her child. Now there was, at this time, a very powerful monarch on the throne in Syria and Phœnicia, named Antiochus. His capital was Damascus. He was wealthy and powerful, and was involved in some difficulties with the Romans. Their conquests, gradually extending eastward, had approached the confines of Antiochus's realms, and the two nations were on the brink of war.

Things being in this state, the enemies of Hannibal at Carthage sent information to the Roman senate that he was negotiating and plotting with Antiochus to combine the Syrian and Carthaginian forces against them, and thus plunge the world into another general war. The Romans accordingly determined to send an embassage to the Carthaginian government, and to demand that Hannibal should be deposed from his office, and given up to them a prisoner, in order that he might be tried on this charge.

These commissioners came, accordingly, to Carthage, keeping, however, the object of their mission a profound secret, since they knew very well that, if Hannibal should suspect it, he would make his escape before the Carthaginian senate could decide upon the question of surrendering him. Hannibal was, however, too wary for them. He contrived to learn their object, and immediately resolved on making his escape. He knew that his enemies in Carthage were numerous and powerful, and that the animosity against him was growing stronger and stronger. He did not dare, therefore, to trust to the result of the discussion in the senate, but determined to fly.

He had a small castle or tower on the coast, about one hundred and fifty miles southeast of Carthage. He sent there by an express, ordering a vessel to be ready to take him to sea. He also made arrangements to have horsemen ready at one of the gates of the city at nightfall. During the day he appeared freely in the public streets, walking with an unconcerned air, as if his mind was at ease, and giving to the Roman embassadors, who were watching his movements, the impression that he was not meditating an escape. Toward the close of the day, however, after walking leisurely home, he immediately made preparations for his journey. As soon as it was dark he went to the gate of the city, mounted the horse which was provided for him, and fled across the country to his castle. Here he found the vessel ready which he had ordered. He embarked, and put to sea.

There is a small island called Cercina at a little distance from the coast. Hannibal reached this island on the same day that he left his tower. There was a harbor here, where merchant ships were accustomed to come in. He found several Phœnician vessels in the port, some bound to Carthage. Hannibal's arrival produced a strong sensation here, and, to account for his appearance among them, he said he was going on an embassy from the Carthaginian government to Tyre.

He was now afraid that some of these vessels that were about setting sail for Carthage might carry the news back of his having being seen at Cercina, and, to prevent this, he contrived, with his characteristic cunning, the following plan: He sent around to all the ship-masters in the port, inviting them to a great entertainment which he was to give, and asked, at the same time, that they would lend him the main-sails of their ships, to make a great awning with, to shelter the guests from the dews of the night. The ship- masters, eager to witness and enjoy the convivial scene which Hannibal's proposal promised them, accepted the invitation, and ordered their main-sails to be taken down. Of course, this confined all their vessels to port. In the evening, the company assembled under the vast tent, made by the main-sails, on the shore. Hannibal met them, and remained with them for a time. In the course of the night, however, when they were all in the midst of their carousing, he stole away, embarked on board a ship, and set sail, and, before the ship-masters could awake from the deep and prolonged slumbers which followed their wine, and rig their main-sails to the masts again, Hannibal was far out of reach on his way to Syria.

In the mean time, there was a great excitement produced at Carthage by the news which spread every where over the city, the day after his departure, that he was not to be found. Great crowds assembled before his house. Wild and strange rumors circulated in explanation of his disappearance, but they were contradictory and impossible, and only added to the universal excitement. This excitement continued until the vessels at last arrived from Cercina, and made the truth known. Hannibal was himself, however, by this time, safe beyond the reach of all possible pursuit. He was sailing prosperously, so far as outward circumstances were concerned, but dejected and wretched in heart, toward Tyre. He landed there in safety, and was kindly received. In a few days he went into the interior, and, after various wanderings, reached Ephesus, where he found Antiochus, the Syrian king.

As soon as the escape of Hannibal was made known at Carthage, the people of the city immediately began to fear that the Romans would consider them responsible for it, and that they should thus incur a renewal of Roman hostility. In order to avert this danger, they immediately sent a deputation to Rome, to make known the fact of Hannibal's flight, and to express the regret they felt on account of it, in hopes thus to save themselves from the displeasure of their formidable foes. It may at first view seem very ungenerous and ungrateful, in the Carthaginians to abandon their general in this manner, in the hour of his misfortune and calamity, and to take part against him with enemies whose displeasure he had incurred only in their service and in executing their will. And this conduct of the Carthaginians would have to be considered as not only ungenerous, but extremely inconsistent, if it had been the same individuals that acted in the two cases. But it was not. The men and the influences which now opposed Hannibal's projects and plans had opposed them always and from the beginning; only, so long as he went on successfully and well, they were in the minority, and Hannibal's adherents and friends controlled all the public action of the city. But, now that the bitter fruits of his ambition and of his totally unjustifiable encroachments on the Roman territories and Roman rights began to be realized, the party of his friends was overturned, the power reverted to the hands of those who had always opposed him, and in trying to keep him down when he was once fallen, their action, whether politically right or wrong, was consistent with itself, and can not be considered as at all subjecting them to the charge of ingratitude or treachery.

One might have supposed that all Hannibal's hopes and expectations of ever again coping with his great Roman enemy would have been now effectually and finally destroyed, and that hence forth he would have given up his active hostility and would have contented himself with seeking some refuge where he could spend the remainder of his days in peace, satisfied with securing, after such dangers and escapes, his own personal protection from the vengeance of his enemies. But it is hard to quell and subdue such indomitable perseverance and energy as his. He was very little inclined yet to submit to his fate. As soon as he found himself at the court of Antiochus, he began to form new plans for making war against Rome. He proposed to the Syrian monarch to raise a naval force and put it under his charge. He said that if Antiochus would give him a hundred ships and ten or twelve thousand men, he would take the command of the expedition in person, and he did not doubt that he should be able to recover his lost ground, and once more humble his ancient and formidable enemy. He would go first, he said, with his force to Carthage, to get the co-operation and aid of his countrymen there in his new plans. Then he would make a descent upon Italy, and he had no doubt that he should soon regain the ascendancy there which he had formerly held.

Hannibal's design of going first to Carthage with his Syrian army was doubtless induced by his desire to put down the party of his enemies there, and to restore the power to his adherents and partisans. In order to prepare the way the more effectually for this, he sent a secret messenger to Carthage, while his negotiations with Antiochus were going on, to make known to his friends there the new hopes which he began to cherish, and the new designs which he had formed. He knew that his enemies in Carthage would be watching very carefully for any such communication; he therefore wrote no letters, and committed nothing to paper which, on being discovered, might betray him. He explained, however, all his plans very fully to his messenger, and gave him minute and careful instructions as to his manner of communicating them.

The Carthaginian authorities were indeed watching very vigilantly, and intelligence was brought to them, by their spies, of the arrival of this stranger. They immediately took measures for arresting him. The messenger, who was himself as vigilant as they, got intelligence of this in his secret lurking-place in the city, and determined immediately to fly. He, however, first prepared some papers and placards, which he posted up in public places, in which he proclaimed that Hannibal was far from considering himself finally conquered; that he was, on the contrary, forming new plans for putting down his enemies in Carthage, resuming his former ascendancy there, and carrying fire and sword again into the Roman territories; and, in the mean time he urged the friends of Hannibal in Carthage to remain faithful and true to his cause.

The messenger, after posting his placards, fled from the city in the night, and went back to Hannibal. Of course, the occurrence produced considerable excitement in the city. It aroused the anger and resentment of Hannibal's enemies, and awakened new encouragement and hope in the hearts of his friends. Further than this, however, it led to no immediate results. The power of the party which was opposed to Hannibal was too firmly established at Carthage to be very easily shaken. They sent information to Rome of the coming of Hannibal's emissary to Carthage, and of the result of his mission, and then every thing went on as before.

In the mean time, the Romans, when they learned where Hannibal had gone, sent two or three commissioners there to confer with the Syrian government in respect to their intentions and plans, and watch the movements of Hannibal. It was said that Scipio himself was joined to this embassy, and that he actually met Hannibal at Ephesus, and had several personal interviews and conversations with him there. Some ancient historian gives a particular account of one of these interviews, in which the conversation turned, as it naturally would do between two such distinguished commanders, on military greatness and glory. Scipio asked Hannibal whom he considered the greatest military hero that had ever lived. Hannibal gave the palm to Alexander the Great, because he had penetrated, with comparatively a very small number of Macedonian troops, into such remote regions, conquered such vast armies, and brought so boundless an empire under his sway. Scipio then asked him who he was inclined to place next to Alexander. He said Pyrrhus. Pyrrhus was a Grecian, who crossed the Adriatic Sea, and made war, with great success, against the Romans. Hannibal said that he gave the second rank to Pyrrhus because he systematized and perfected the art of war, and also because he had the power of awakening a feeling of personal attachment to himself on the part of all his soldiers, and even of the inhabitants of the countries that he conquered, beyond any other general that ever lived. Scipio then asked Hannibal who came next in order, and he replied that he should give the third rank to himself. "And if," added he, "I had conquered Scipio, I should consider myself as standing above Alexander, Pyrrhus, and all the generals that the world ever produced."

Various other anecdotes are related of Hannibal during the time of his first appearance in Syria, all indicating the very high degree of estimation in which he was held, and the curiosity, and interest that were every where felt to see him. On one occasion, it happened that a vain and self-conceited orator, who knew little of war but from his own theoretic speculations, was haranguing an assembly where Hannibal was present, being greatly pleased with the opportunity of displaying his powers before so distinguished an auditor. When the discourse was finished, they asked Hannibal what he thought of it. "I have heard," said he, in reply, "many old dotards in the course of my life, but this is, verily, the greatest dotard of them all."

Hannibal failed, notwithstanding all his perseverance, in obtaining the means to attack the Romans again. He was unwearied in his efforts, but, though the king sometimes encouraged his hopes, nothing was ever done. He remained in this part of the world for ten years, striving continually to accomplish his aims, but every year he found himself further from the attainment of them than ever. The hour of his good fortune and of his prosperity were obviously gone. His plans all failed, his influence declined, his name and renown were fast passing away. At last, after long and fruitless contests with the Romans, Antiochus made a treaty of peace with them, and, among the articles of this treaty, was one agreeing to give up Hannibal into their power.

Hannibal resolved to fly. The place of refuge which he chose was the island of Crete. He found that he could not long remain here. He had, however, brought with him a large amount of treasure, and when about leaving Crete again, he was uneasy about this treasure, as he had some reason to fear that the Cretans were intending to seize it. He must contrive, then, some stratagem to enable him to get this gold away. The plan he adopted was this:

He filled a number of earthen jars with lead, covering the tops of them with gold and silver. These he carried, with great appearance of caution and solicitude, to the Temple of Diana, a very sacred edifice, and deposited them there, under very special guardianship of the Cretans, to whom, as he said, he intrusted all his treasures. They received their false deposit with many promises to keep it safely, and then Hannibal went away with his real gold cast in the center of hollow statues of brass, which he carried with him, without suspicion, as objects of art of very little value.

Hannibal fled from kingdom to kingdom, and from province to province, until life became a miserable burden. The determined hostility of the Roman senate followed him every where, harassing him with continual anxiety and fear, and destroying all hope of comfort and peace. His mind was a prey to bitter recollections of the past, and still more dreadful forebodings for the future. He had spent all the morning of his life in inflicting the most terrible injuries on the objects of his implacable animosity and hate, although they had never injured him, and now, in the evening of his days, it became his destiny to feel the pressure of the same terror and suffering inflicted upon him. The hostility which he had to fear was equally merciless with that which he had exercised; perhaps it was made still more intense by being mingled with what they who felt it probably considered a just resentment and revenge.

When at length Hannibal found that the Romans were hemming him in more and more closely, and that the danger increased of his falling at last into their power, he had a potion of poison prepared, and kept it always in readiness, determined to die by his own hand rather than to submit to be given up to his enemies. The time for taking the poison at last arrived. The wretched fugitive was then in Bithynia, a kingdom of Asia Minor. The King of Bithynia sheltered him for a time, but at length agreed to give him up to the Romans. Hannibal, learning this, prepared for flight. But he found, on attempting his escape, that all the modes of exit from the palace which he occupied, even the secret ones which he had expressly contrived to aid his flight, were taken possession of and guarded. Escape was, therefore, no longer possible, and Hannibal went to his apartment and sent for the poison. He was now an old man, nearly seventy years of age, and he was worn down and exhausted by his protracted anxieties and sufferings. He was glad to die. He drank the poison, and in a few hours ceased to breathe.

12

The Destruction of Carthage

THE consequences of Hannibal's reckless ambition, and of his wholly unjustifiable aggression on Roman rights to gratify it, did not end with his own personal ruin. The flame which he had kindled continued to burn until at last it accomplished the entire and irretrievable destruction of Carthage.

This was effected in a third and final war between the Carthaginians and the Romans, which is known in history as the third Punic war. With a narrative of the events of this war, ending, as it did, in the total destruction of the city, we shall close this history of Hannibal.

It will be recollected that the war which Hannibal himself waged against Rome was the second in the series, the contest in which Regulus figured so prominently having been the first. The one whose history is now to be given is the third. The reader will distinctly understand the chronological relations of these contests by the table on the following page:

Date B.C.	Event	Punic War
264	War commenced in Italy	
262	Naval battles in Mediterranean	I.
249	Regulus sent prisoner to Rome	24 years.
241	Peace concluded	
	Peace for 22 years.	
219	Hannibal attacks Saguntum	
218	Crosses the Alps	
216	Battle of Cannæ	II.
205	Is conquered by Scipio	17 years.
200	Peace concluded	
	Peace for 52 years.	
148	War declared	II.
146	Carthage destroyed	3 years.

These three Punic wars extended, as the table shows, over a period of more than a hundred years. Each successive contest in the series was shorter, but more violent and desperate than its predecessor, while the intervals of peace were longer. Thus the first Punic war continued for twenty-four years, the second about seventeen, and the third only three or four. The interval, too, between the first and second was twenty-four years, while between the second and third there was a sort of peace for about fifty years. These differences were caused, indeed, in some degree, by the accidental circumstances on which the successive ruptures depended, but they were not entirely owing to that cause. The longer these belligerent relations between the two countries continued, and the more they both experienced the awful effects and consequences of their quarrels, the less disposed they were to renew such dreadful struggles, and yet, when they did renew them, they engaged in them with redoubled energy of determination and fresh intensity of hate. Thus, the wars followed each other at greater intervals, but the conflicts, when they came, though shorter in duration, were more and more desperate and merciless in character.

We have said that, after the close of the second Punic war, there was a sort of peace for about fifty years. Of course, during this time, one generation after another of public men arose, both in Rome and Carthage, each successive group, on both sides, inheriting the suppressed animosity and hatred which had been cherished by their predecessors. Of course, as long as Hannibal had lived, and had continued his plots and schemes in Syria, he was the means of keeping up a continual irritation among the people of Rome against the Carthaginian name. It is true that the government at Carthage disavowed his acts, and professed to be wholly opposed to his designs; but then it was, of course, very well known at Rome that this was only because they thought he was not able to execute them. They had no confidence whatever in Carthaginian faith or honesty, and, of course, there could be no real harmony or stable peace.

There arose, gradually, also, another source of dissension. By referring to the map, the reader will perceive that there lies, to the westward of Carthage, a country called Numidia. This country was a hundred miles or more in breadth, and extended back several hundred miles into the interior. It was a very rich and fertile region, and contained many powerful and wealthy cities. The inhabitants were warlike, too, and were particularly celebrated for their cavalry. The ancient historians say that they used to ride their horses into the field without saddles, and often without bridles, guiding and controlling them by their voices, and keeping their seats securely by the exercise of great personal strength and consummate skill. These Numidian horsemen are often alluded to in the narratives of Hannibal's campaigns, and, in fact, in all the military histories of the times.

Among the kings who reigned in Numidia was one who had taken sides with the Romans in the second Punic war. His name was Masinissa. He became involved in some struggle for power with a neighboring monarch named Syphax, and while he, that is, Masinissa, had allied himself to the Romans, Syphax had joined the Carthaginians, each chieftain hoping, by this means, to gain assistance from his allies in conquering the other. Masinissa's patrons proved to be the strongest, and at the end of the second Punic war, when the conditions of peace were made, Masinissa's dominions were enlarged, and the undisturbed possession of them confirmed to him, the Carthaginians being bound by express stipulations not to molest him in any way.

In commonwealths like those of Rome and Carthage, there will always be two great parties struggling against each other for the possession of power. Each wishes to avail itself of every opportunity to oppose and thwart the other, and they consequently almost always take different sides in all the great questions of public policy that arise. There were two such parties at Rome, and they disagreed in respect to the course which should be pursued in regard to Carthage, one being generally in favor of peace, the other perpetually calling for war. In the same manner there was at Carthage a similar dissension, the one side in the contest being desirous to propitiate the Romans and avoid collisions with them, while the other party were very restless, and uneasy under the pressure of the Roman power upon them, and were endeavoring continually to foment feelings of hostility against their ancient enemies, as if they wished that war should break out again. The latter party were not strong enough to bring the Carthaginian state into an open rupture with Rome itself, but they succeeded at last in getting their government involved in a dispute with Masinissa, and in leading out an army to give him battle.

Fifty years had passed away, as has already been remarked, since the close of Hannibal's war. During this time, Scipio—that is, the Scipio who conquered Hannibal—had disappeared from the stage. Masinissa himself was very far advanced in life, being over eighty years of age. He, however, still retained the strength and energy which had characterized him in his prime. He drew together an immense army, and mounting, like his soldiers, bare-back upon his horse, he rode from rank to rank, gave the necessary commands, and matured the arrangements for battle.

The name of the Carthaginian general on this occasion was Hasdrubal. This was a very common name at Carthage, especially among the friends and family of Hannibal. The bearer of it, in this case, may possibly have received it from his parents in commemoration of the brother of Hannibal, who lost his head in descending into Italy from the Alps, inasmuch as during the fifty years of peace which had elapsed, there was ample time for a child born after that event to grow up to full maturity. At any rate, the new Hasdrubal inherited the inveterate hatred to Rome which characterized his namesake, and he and his party had contrived to gain a temporary ascendancy in Carthage, and they availed themselves of their brief possession of power to renew, indirectly at least, the contest with Rome. They sent the rival leaders into banishment, raised an army, and Hasdrubal himself taking the command of it, they went forth in great force to encounter Masinissa.

It was in a way very similar to this that Hannibal had commenced his war with Rome, by seeking first a quarrel with a Roman ally. Hannibal, it is true, had commenced his aggressions at Saguntum, in Spain. Hasdrubal begins in Numidia, in Africa, but, with the exception of the difference of geographical locality, all seems the same, and Hasdrubal very probably supposed that he was about to enter himself upon the same glorious career which had immortalized his great ancestor's name.

There was another analogy between the two cases; viz., that both Hannibal and Hasdrubal had strong parties opposed to them in Carthage in the incipient stages of their undertakings. In the present instance, the opposition had been violently suppressed, and the leaders of it sent into banishment; but still the elements remained, ready, in case of any disaster to Hasdrubal's arms, or any other occurrence tending to diminish his power, to rise at once and put him down. Hasdrubal had therefore a double enemy to contend against: one before him, on the battle-field, and the other, perhaps still more formidable, in the city behind him.

The parallel, however, ends here. Hannibal conquered at Saguntum, but Hasdrubal was entirely defeated in the battle in Numidia. The battle was fought long and desperately on both sides, but the Carthaginians were obliged to yield, and they retreated at length in confusion to seek shelter in their camp. The battle was witnessed by a Roman officer who stood upon a neighboring hill, and looked down upon the scene with intense interest all the day. It was Scipio—the younger Scipio—who became afterward the principal actor in the terrible scenes which were enacted in the war which followed. He was then a distinguished officer in the Roman army, and was on duty in Spain. His commanding general there had sent him to Africa to procure some elephants from Masinissa for the use of the army. He came to Numidia, accordingly, for this purpose, and as the battle between Masinissa and Hasdrubal came while he was there, he remained to witness it.

This second Scipio was not, by blood, any relative of the other, but he had been adopted by the elder Scipio's son, and thus received his name; so that he was, by adoption, a grandson. He was, even at this time, a man of high consideration among all who knew him, for his great energy and efficiency of character, as well as for his sound judgment and practical good sense. He occupied a very singular position at the time of this battle, such as very few great commanders have ever been placed in; for, as he himself was attached to a Roman army in Spain, having been sent merely as a military messenger to Numidia, he was a neutral in this contest, and, could not, properly, take part on either side. He had, accordingly, only to take his place upon the hill, and look down upon the awful scene as upon a spectacle arranged for his special gratification. He speaks of it as if he were highly gratified with the opportunity he enjoyed, saying that only two such cases had ever occurred before, where a general could look down, in such a way, upon a great battlefield, and witness the whole progress of the fight, himself a cool and disinterested spectator. He was greatly excited by the scene, and he speaks particularly of the appearance of the veteran Masinissa, then eighty-four years old, who rode all day from rank to rank, on a wild and impetuous charger, without a saddle, to give his orders to his men, and to encourage and animate them by his voice and his example.

Hasdrubal retreated with his forces to his camp as soon as the battle was over, and intrenched himself there, while Masinissa advanced with his army, surrounded the encampment, and hemmed the imprisoned fugitives in. Finding himself in extreme and imminent danger, Hasdrubal sent to Masinissa to open negotiations for peace, and he proposed that Scipio should act as a sort of umpire or mediator between the two parties, to arrange the terms. Scipio was not likely to be a very impartial umpire; but still, his interposition would afford him, as Hasdrubal thought, some protection against any excessive and extreme exorbitancy on the part of his conqueror. The plan, however, did not succeed. Even Scipio's terms were found by Hasdrubal to be inadmissible. He required that the Carthaginians should accord to Masinissa a certain extension of territory. Hasdrubal was willing to assent to this. They were to pay him, also, a large sum of money. He agreed, also, to this. They were, moreover, to allow Hasdrubal's banished opponents to return to Carthage. This, by putting the party opposed to Hasdrubal once more into power in Carthage, would have been followed by his own fall and ruin; he could not consent to it. He remained, therefore, shut up in his camp, and Scipio, giving up the hope of effecting an accommodation, took the elephants which had been provided for him, and returned across the Mediterranean to Spain.

Soon after this, Hasdrubal's army, worn out with hunger and misery in their camp, compelled him to surrender on Masinissa's own terms. The men were allowed to go free, but most of them perished on the way to Carthage. Hasdrubal himself succeeded in reaching some place of safety, but the influence of his party was destroyed by the disastrous result of his enterprise, and his exiled enemies being recalled in accordance with the treaty of surrender, the opposing party were immediately restored to power.

Under these new councils, the first measure of the Carthaginians was to impeach Hasdrubal on a charge of treason, for having involved his country in these difficulties, and the next was to send a solemn embassy to Rome, to acknowledge the fault of which their nation had been guilty, to offer to surrender Hasdrubal into their hands, as the principal author of the deed, and to ask what further satisfaction the Romans demanded.

In the mean time, before these messengers arrived, the Romans had been deliberating what to do. The strongest party were in favor of urging on the quarrel with Carthage and declaring war. They had not, however, come to any positive decision. They received the deputation, therefore, very coolly, and made them no direct reply. As to the satisfaction which the Carthaginians ought to render to the Romans for having made war upon their ally contrary to the solemn covenants of the treaty, they said that that was a question for the Carthaginians themselves to consider. They had nothing at present to say upon the subject. The deputies returned to Carthage with this reply, which, of course, produced great uneasiness and anxiety.

The Carthaginians were more and more desirous now to do every thing in their power to avert the threatened danger of Roman hostility. They sent a new embassy to Rome, with still more humble professions than before. The embassy set sail from Carthage with very little hope, however, of accomplishing the object of their mission. They were authorized, nevertheless, to make the most unlimited concessions, and to submit to any conditions whatever to avert the calamity of another war.

But the Romans had been furnished with a pretext for commencing hostilities again, and there was a very strong party among them now who were determined to avail themselves of this opportunity to extinguish entirely the Carthaginian power. War had, accordingly, been declared by the Roman senate very soon after the first embassy had returned, a fleet and army had been raised and equipped, and the expedition had sailed. When, therefore, the embassy arrived in Rome, they found that the war, which it was the object of their mission to avert, had been declared.

The Romans, however, gave them audience. The embassadors expressed their willingness to submit to any terms that the senate might propose for arresting the war. The senate replied that they were willing to make a treaty with the Carthaginians, on condition that the latter were to surrender themselves entirely to the Roman power, and bind themselves to obey such orders as the consuls, on their arrival in Africa with the army, should issue; the Romans, on their part, guarantying that they should continue in the enjoyment of their liberty, of their territorial possessions, and of their laws. As proof, however, of the Carthaginian honesty of purpose in making the treaty, and security for their future submission, they were required to give up to the Romans three hundred hostages. These hostages were to be young persons from the first families in Carthage, the sons of the men who were most prominent in society there, and whose influence might be supposed to control the action of the nation. The embassadors could not but consider these as very onerous terms. They did not know what orders the consuls would give them on their arrival in Africa, and they were required to put the commonwealth wholly into their power. Besides, in the guarantee which the Romans offered them, their territories and their laws were to be protected, but nothing was said of their cities, their ships, or their arms and munitions of war. The agreement there, if executed, would put the Carthaginian commonwealth wholly at the mercy of their masters, in respect to all those things which were in those days most valuable to a nation as elements of power. Still, the embassadors had been instructed to make peace with the Romans on any terms, and they accordingly acceded to these, though with great reluctance. They were especially averse to the agreement in respect to the hostages.

This system, which prevailed universally in ancient times, of having the government of one nation surrender the children of the most distinguished citizens to that of another, as security for the fulfillment of its treaty stipulations, was a very cruel hardship to those who had to suffer the separation; but it would seem that there was no other security strong enough to hold such lawless powers as governments were in those days, to their word. Stern and rough as the men of those warlike nations often were, mothers were the same then as now, and they suffered quite as keenly in seeing their children sent away from them, to pine in a foreign land, in hopeless exile, for many years; in danger, too, continually, of the most cruel treatment, and even of death itself, to revenge some alleged governmental wrong.

Of course, the embassadors knew, when they returned to Carthage with these terms, that they were bringing heavy tidings. The news, in fact, when it came, threw the community into the most extreme distress. It is said that the whole city was filled with cries and lamentations. The mothers, who felt that they were about to be bereaved, beat their breasts, and tore their hair, and manifested by every other sign their extreme and unmitigated woe. They begged and entreated their husbands and fathers not to consent to such cruel and intolerable conditions. They could not, and they would not give up their children.

The husbands and the fathers, however, felt compelled to resist all these entreaties. They could not now undertake to resist the Roman will. Their army had been well-nigh destroyed in the battle with Masinissa; their city was consequently defenseless, and the Roman fleet had already reached its African port, and the troops were landed. There was no possible way, it appeared, of saving themselves and their city from absolute destruction, but entire submission to the terms which their stern conquerors had imposed upon them.

The hostages were required to be sent, within thirty days, to the island of Sicily, to a port on the western extremity of the island, called Lilybæum. Lilybæum was the port in Sicily nearest to Carthage, being perhaps at a distance of a hundred miles across the waters of the Mediterranean Sea. A Roman escort was to be ready to receive them there and conduct them to Rome. Although thirty days were allowed to the Carthaginians to select and send forward the hostages, they determined not to avail themselves of this offered delay, but to send the unhappy children forward at once, that they might testify to the Roman senate, by this their promptness, that they were very earnestly desirous to propitiate their favor.

The children were accordingly designated, one from each of the leading families in the city, and three hundred in all. The reader must imagine the heart-rending scenes of suffering which must have desolated these three hundred families and homes, when the stern and inexorable edict came to each of them that one loved member of the household must be selected to go. And when, at last, the hour arrived for their departure, and they assembled upon the pier, the picture was one of intense and unmingled suffering. The poor exiles stood bewildered with terror and grief, about to part with all that they ever held dear—their parents, their brothers and sisters, and their native land—to go they knew not whither, under the care of iron-hearted soldiers, who seemed to know no feelings of tenderness or compassion for their woes. Their disconsolate mothers wept and groaned aloud, clasping the loved ones who were about to be torn forever from them in their arms, in a delirium of maternal affection and irrepressible grief; their brothers and sisters, and their youthful friends stood by, some almost frantic with emotions which they did not attempt to suppress, others mute and motionless in their sorrow, shedding bitter tears of anguish, or gazing wildly on the scene with looks of despair; while the fathers, whose stern duty it was to pass through this scene unmoved, walked to and fro restlessly, in deep but silent distress, spoke in broken and incoherent words to one another, and finally aided, by a mixture of persuasion and gentle force, in drawing the children away from their mothers' arms, and getting them on board the vessels which were to convey them away. The vessels made sail, and passed off slowly from the shore. The mothers watched them till they could no longer be seen, and then returned, disconsolate and wretched, to their homes; and then the grief and agitation of this parting scene was succeeded by the anxious suspense which now pervaded the whole city to learn what new dangers and indignities they were to suffer from the approaching Roman army, which they knew must now be well on its way.

The Roman army landed at Utica. Utica was a large city to the north of Carthage, not far from it, and upon the same bay. When the people of Utica found that another serious collision was to take place between Rome and Carthage, they had foreseen what would probably be the end of the contest, and they had decided that, in order to save themselves from the ruin which was plainly impending over the sister city, they must abandon her to her fate, and make common cause with Rome. They had, accordingly, sent deputies to the Roman senate, offering to surrender Utica to their power. The Romans had accepted the submission, and had made this city, in consequence, the port of debarkation for their army.

As soon as the news arrived at Carthage that the Roman army had landed at Utica, the people sent deputies to inquire what were the orders of the consuls, for it will be recollected they had bound themselves by the treaty to obey the orders which the consuls were to bring. They found, when they arrived there, that the bay was covered with the Roman shipping. There were fifty vessels of war, of three banks of oars each, and a vast number of transports besides. There was, too, in the camp upon the shore, a force of eighty thousand foot soldiers and four thousand horse, all armed and equipped in the most perfect manner.

The deputies were convinced that this was a force which it was in vain for their countrymen to think of resisting. They asked, trembling, for the consuls' orders. The consuls informed them that the orders of the Roman senate were, first, that the Carthaginians should furnish them with a supply of corn for the subsistence of their troops. The deputies went back to Carthage with the demand.

The Carthaginians resolved to comply. They were bound by their treaty and by the hostages they had given, as well as intimidated by the presence of the Roman force. They furnished the corn.

The consuls, soon after this, made another demand of the Carthaginians. It was, that they should surrender to them all their vessels of war. They were more unwilling to comply with this requisition than with the other; but they assented at last. They hoped that the demands of their enemies would stop here, and that, satisfied with having weakened them thus far, they would go away and leave them; they could then build new ships again when better times should return.

But the Romans were not satisfied yet. They sent a third order, that the Carthaginians should deliver up all their arms, military stores, and warlike machines of every kind, by sending them into the Roman camp. The Carthaginians were rendered almost desperate by this requisition. Many were determined that they would not submit to it, but would resist at all hazards. Others despaired of all possibility of resisting now, and gave up all as lost; while the three hundred families from which the hostages had gone, trembled for the safety of the captive children, and urged compliance with the demand. The advocates for submission finally gained the day. The arms were collected, and carried in an immensely long train of wagons to the Roman camp. There were two hundred thousand complete suits of armor, with darts and javelins without number, and two thousand military engines for hurling beams of wood and stones. Thus Carthage was disarmed.

All these demands, however unreasonable and cruel as the Carthaginians deemed them, were only preliminary to the great final determination, the announcement of which the consuls had reserved for the end. When the arms had all been delivered, the consuls announced to their now defenseless victims that the Roman senate had come to the determination that Carthage was to be destroyed. They gave orders, accordingly, that the inhabitants should all leave the city, which, as soon as it should be thus vacated, was to be burned. They might take with them such property as they could carry; and they were at liberty to build, in lieu of their fortified sea-port, an inland town, not less than ten miles' distance from the sea, only it must have no walls or fortifications of any kind. As soon as the inhabitants were gone, Carthage, the consuls said, was to be destroyed.

The announcement of this entirely unparalleled and intolerable requisition threw the whole city into a phrensy of desperation. They could not, and would not, submit to this. The entreaties and remonstrances of the friends of the hostages were all silenced or overborne in the burst of indignation and anger which arose from the whole city. The gates were closed. The pavements of the streets were torn up, and buildings demolished to obtain stones, which were carried up upon the ramparts to serve instead of weapons. The slaves were all liberated, and stationed on the walls to aid in the defense. Every body that could work at a forge was employed in fabricating swords, spearheads, pikes, and such other weapons as could be formed with the greatest facility and dispatch. They used all the iron and brass that could be obtained, and then melted down vases and statues of the precious metals, and tipped their spears with an inferior pointing of silver and gold. In the same manner, when the supplies of flax and hempen twine for cordage for their bows failed, the beautiful sisters and mothers of the hostages cut off their long hair, and twisted and braided it into cords to be used as bow-strings for propelling the arrows which their husbands and brothers made. In a word, the wretched Carthaginians had been pushed beyond the last limit of human endurance, and had aroused themselves to a hopeless resistance in a sort of phrensy of despair.

The reader will recollect that, after the battle with Masinissa, Hasdrubal lost all his influence in Carthage, and was, to all appearance, hopelessly ruined. He had not, however, then given up the struggle. He had contrived to assemble the remnant of his army in the neighborhood of Carthage. His forces had been gradually increasing during these transactions, as those who were opposed to these concessions to the Romans naturally gathered around him. He was now in his camp, not far from the city, at the head of twenty thousand men. Finding themselves in so desperate an emergency, the Carthaginians sent to him to come to their succor. He very gladly obeyed the summons. He sent around to all the territories still subject to Carthage, and gathered fresh troops, and collected supplies of arms and of food. He advanced to the relief of the city. He compelled the Romans, who were equally astonished at the resistance they met with from within the walls, and at this formidable onset from without, to retire a little, and intrench themselves in their camp, in order to secure their own safety. He sent supplies of food into the city. He also contrived to fit up, secretly, a great many fire-ships in the harbor, and setting them in flames, let them drift down upon the Roman fleet, which was anchored in supposed security in the bay. The plan was so skillfully managed that the Roman ships were almost all destroyed. Thus the face of affairs was changed. The Romans found themselves disappointed for the present of their prey. They confined themselves to their encampment, and sent home to the Roman senate for new re-enforcements and supplies.

In a word, the Romans found that, instead of having only to effect, unresisted, the simple destruction of a city, they were involved in what would, perhaps, prove a serious and a protracted war. The war did, in fact, continue for two or three years—a horrible war, almost of extermination, on both sides. Scipio came with the Roman army, at first as a subordinate officer; but his bravery, his sagacity, and the success of some of his almost romantic exploits, soon made him an object of universal regard. At one time, a detachment of the army, which, he succeeded in releasing from a situation of great peril in which they had been placed, testified their gratitude by platting a crown of grass, and placing it upon his brow with great ceremony and loud acclamations.

The Carthaginians did every thing in the prosecution of this war that the most desperate valor could do; but Scipio's cool, steady, and well-calculated plans made irresistible progress, and hemmed them in at last, within narrower and narrower limits, by a steadily-increasing pressure, from which they found it impossible to break away.

Scipio had erected a sort of mole or pier upon the water near the city, on which he had erected many large and powerful engines to assault the walls. One night a large company of Carthaginians took torches, not lighted, in their hands, together with some sort of apparatus for striking fire, and partly by wading and partly by swimming, they made their way through the water of the harbor toward these machines. When they were sufficiently near, they struck their lights and set their torches on fire. The Roman soldiers who had been stationed to guard the machines were seized with terror at seeing all these flashing fires burst out suddenly over the surface of the water, and fled in dismay. The Carthaginians set the abandoned engines on fire, and then, throwing their now useless torches into the flames, plunged into the water again, and swam back in safety. But all this desperate bravery did very little good. Scipio quietly repaired the engines, and the siege went on as before.

But we can not describe in detail all the particulars of this protracted and terrible struggle. We must pass on to the closing scene, which, as related by the historians of the day, is an almost incredible series of horrors. After an immense number had been killed in the assaults which had been made upon the city, besides the thousands and thousands which had died of famine, and of the exposures and hardships incident to such a siege, the army of Scipio succeeded in breaking their way through the gates, and gaining admission to the city. Some of the inhabitants were now disposed to contend no longer, but to cast themselves at the mercy of the conqueror. Others, furious in their despair, were determined to fight to the last, not willing to give up the pleasure of killing all they could of their hated enemies, even to save their lives. They fought, therefore, from street to street, retreating gradually as the Romans advanced, till they found refuge in the citadel. One band of Scipio's soldiers mounted to the tops of the houses, the roofs being flat, and fought their way there, while another column advanced in the same manner in the streets below. No imagination can conceive the uproar and din of such an assault upon a populous city—a horrid mingling of the vociferated commands of the officers, and of the shouts of the advancing and victorious assailants, with the screams of terror from affrighted women and children, and dreadful groans and imprecations from men dying maddened with unsatisfied revenge, and biting the dust in an agony of pain.

The more determined of the combatants, with Hasdrubal at their head, took possession of the citadel, which was a quarter of the city situated upon an eminence, and strongly fortified. Scipio advanced to the walls of this fortification, and set that part of the city on fire which lay nearest to it. The fire burned for six days, and opened a large area, which afforded the Roman troops room to act. When the troops were brought up to the area thus left vacant by the fire, and the people within the citadel saw that their condition was hopeless, there arose, as there always does in such cases, the desperate struggle within the walls whether to persist in resistance or to surrender in despair. There was an immense mass, not far from sixty thousand, half women and children, who were determined on going out to surrender themselves to Scipio's mercy, and beg for their lives. Hasdrubal's wife, leading her two children by her side, earnestly entreated her husband to allow her to go with them. But he refused. There was a body of deserters from the Roman camp in the citadel, who, having no possible hope of escaping destruction except by desperate resistance to the last, Hasdrubal supposed would never yield. He committed his wife and children, therefore, to their charge, and these deserters, seeking refuge in a great temple within the citadel, bore the frantic mother with them to share their fate.

Hasdrubal's determination, however, to resist the Romans to the last, soon after this gave way, and he determined to surrender. He is accused of the most atrocious treachery in attempting thus to save himself, after excluding his wife and children from all possibility of escaping destruction. But the confusion and din of such a scene, the suddenness and violence with which the events succeed each other, and the tumultuous and uncontrollable mental agitation to which they give rise, deprive a man who is called to act in it of all sense and reason, and exonerate him, almost as much, from moral responsibility for what he does, as if he were insane. At any rate, Hasdrubal, after shutting up his wife and children with a furious gang of desperadoes who could not possibly surrender, surrendered himself, perhaps hoping that he might save them after all.

The Carthaginian soldiers, following Hasdrubal's example, opened the gates of the citadel, and let the conqueror in. The deserters were now made absolutely desperate by their danger, and some of them, more furious than the rest, preferring to die by their own hands rather than to give their hated enemies the pleasure of killing them, set the building in which they were shut up in on fire. The miserable inmates ran to and fro, half suffocated by the smoke and scorched by the flames. Many of them reached the roof. Hasdrubal's wife and children were among the number. She looked down from this elevation, the volumes of smoke and flame rolling up around her, and saw her husband standing below with the Roman general—perhaps looking, in consternation, for his wife and children, amid this scene of horror. The sight of the husband and father in a position of safety made the wife and mother perfectly furious with resentment and anger. "Wretch!" she screamed, in a voice which raised itself above the universal din, "is it thus you seek to save your own life while you sacrifice ours? I can not reach you in your own person, but I kill you hereby in the persons of your children." So saying, she stabbed her affrighted sons with a dagger, and hurled them down, struggling all the time against their insane mother's phrensy, into the nearest opening from which flames were ascending, and then leaped in after them herself to share their awful doom.

The Romans, when they had gained possession of the city, took most effectual measures for its complete destruction. The inhabitants were scattered into the surrounding country, and the whole territory was converted into a Roman province. Some attempts were afterward made to rebuild the city, and it was for a long time a place of some resort, as men lingered mournfully there in huts that they built among the ruins. It, however, was gradually forsaken, the stones crumbled and decayed, vegetation regained, possession of the soil, and now there is nothing whatever to mark the spot where the city lay.

War and commerce are the two great antagonistic principles which struggle for the mastery of the human race, the function of the one being to preserve, and that of the other to destroy. Commerce causes cities to be built and fields to be cultivated, and diffuses comfort and plenty, and all the blessings of industry and peace. It carries organization and order every where; it protects property and life; it disarms pestilence, and it prohibits famine. War, on the other hand, destroys. It disorganizes the social state. It ruins cities, depopulates fields, condemns men to idleness and want, and the only remedy it knows for the evils which it brings upon man is to shorten the miseries of its victims by giving pestilence and famine the most ample commission to destroy their lives.

Thus war is the great enemy, while commerce is the great friend of humanity. They are antagonistic principles, contending continually for the mastery among all the organizations of men.

When Hannibal appeared upon the stage, he found his country engaged peacefully and prosperously in exchanging the productions of the various countries of the then known world, and promoting every where the comfort and happiness of mankind. He contrived to turn all these energies into the new current of military aggression, conquest, and war. He perfectly succeeded. We certainly have in his person and history all the marks and characteristics of a great military hero. He gained the most splendid victories, devastated many lands, embarrassed and stopped the commercial intercourse which was carrying the comforts of life to so many thousand homes, and spread, instead of them, every where, privation, want, and terror, with pestilence and famine in their train. He kept the country of his enemies in a state of incessant anxiety, suffering, and alarm for many years, and overwhelmed his own native land, in the end, in absolute and irresistible ruin. In a word, he was one of the greatest military heroes that the world has ever known.

THE END

ABOUT JACOB ABBOTT

Jacob Abbott was born in Hallowell, Maine in 1803, the son of a minister and farmer. Even as a young boy, he showed academic promise and an interest in spiritual matters. After attending the Hallowell Academy, he was admitted to Bowdoin College at the age of 14.

At Bowdoin, Abbott studied classics and mathematics. He graduated second in his class in 1820 at the young age of 16. He was known as a serious and studious young man who strove for excellence.

After college, Abbott went on to study at Andover Theological Seminary with the intention of becoming a Congregationalist minister. However, his rigorous study habits and frail health caused him to abandon this pursuit after just two years.

Abbott was plagued by gastrointestinal issues and migraines throughout his life, likely exacerbated by the demanding academic environment. His poor health finally forced him to leave his ministerial studies and turn to the less stressful pursuits of writing and tutoring.

First, Abbott took a job as a professor of mathematics and natural philosophy at Amherst College in 1824. The following year, he married Harriet Vaughan and moved to Boston where he opened a school for young ladies. It was during this time that he began writing simple textbooks for teaching science, history and Christian values.

So while Abbott had aspired to be a minister, chronic health issues led him to find an alternate calling educating children through clear and engaging writing. This pivot would launch his successful career as one of the most famous children's authors of the 19th century.

In 1825, Abbott married Harriet Vaughan and soon after started his own school for young ladies in Boston. During this time, he began writing educational books in a popular, simple style. His early works included the Mount Vernon Reader and The Young Christian.

Abbott gained fame with the Rollo series, first published in 1835. These stories followed a young boy named Rollo learning morals and virtues through his everyday adventures. The series was hugely popular and established Abbott's reputation as a gifted children's writer.

Other notable books by Abbott include the Franconia Stories (1853-1873), a 10-volume series about a brother and sister's adventures in the country, and the Marco Paul series (1853-1873), which followed a boy's travels around America learning about each state.

In all, Jacob Abbott wrote over 200 books, primarily for young readers. His works were praised for their ability to educate and impart moral lessons in an engaging, story-driven way. Though largely forgotten today, he was one of the most prolific and beloved children's authors of his era.

Abbott continued writing up until his death on October 31, 1879 in Farmington, Maine. His legacy lives on through his contributions to 19th century children's literature.

BIOGRAPHIES ABBOTT WROTE

A number of the books Abbott wrote were biographies of famous people. Famous characters covered in these books included:

Alexander the Great: This book provides a sweeping look at the life and achievements of Alexander III of Macedon, better known as Alexander the Great. It follows his early education by Aristotle, ascension to the throne after his father Philip II's assassination, and extensive military campaigns across Asia and northeast Africa. Abbott recounts Alexander's major battles against the Persians and annexation of their empire. The book also examines Alexander's tactics, military innovations, and creation of a Hellenistic empire stretching from Greece to India before his death at 32.

Alfred the Great: This biography focuses on Alfred's defense of the Kingdom of Wessex against Viking raids in 9th century England. It discusses how Alfred drove back the Great Heathen Army and then negotiated terms with the Vikings, designating parts of England for their settlement. Abbott also highlights Alfred's efforts to revive learning and education in England, as well as his codification of laws and strengthening of the Anglo-Saxon navy. The book frames Alfred as a scholarly, strategic and devout ruler whose achievements laid the foundation for a unified England.

King Charles I: This book looks at the reign of Charles I leading up to and during the English Civil War. It focuses on the religious and political conflicts between Charles I and Parliament, caused largely by

Charles' belief in divine right of kings and many unpopular, authoritarian policies. Abbott also examines Charles' refusal to compromise, leading to the war against Parliament's New Model Army and his eventual execution for treason in 1649 under Oliver Cromwell.

King Charles II: This biography deals with the restoration of the English monarchy under Charles II after the death of Oliver Cromwell. It follows Charles II's return from exile and re-establishment of royal power. However, Abbott also notes Charles' own conflicts with Parliament and religious controversies during his reign. The book discusses Charles' hedonistic lifestyle and many mistresses, but also his support for science, exploration and trade that helped expand the British Empire.

Cleopatra: This book examines Cleopatra VII's life and rule over ancient Egypt. Abbott chronicles Cleopatra's relationships and political alliances with Julius Caesar and Mark Antony, as she sought to maintain Egypt's independence from Rome. The biography highlights Cleopatra's intelligence, education and strategic skills in dealing with Rome. But it ultimately focuses on Cleopatra's downfall and suicide after Mark Antony's defeat by Octavian, leading to Egypt becoming a Roman province.

Cyrus the Great: This biography covers Cyrus II of Persia, founder of the Achaemenid Empire. Abbott traces Cyrus's rise from Persian prince, to revolt against the Medes, to conqueror of the Lydian and Babylonian empires. The book also examines Cyrus's leadership qualities and tolerant policies toward conquered peoples. It portrays Cyrus as a wise, inspirational leader who created the model of a centralized Persian state.

Darius: This book looks at the reign of Darius I, examining his consolidation of the Persian Empire through administrative reforms, development of infrastructure, and expansion of territory. Abbott discusses

Darius's division of the empire into provinces and implementation of a uniform tax system and coinage. The biography also covers his invasion of Greece which was thwarted at the famous Battle of Marathon. Overall, it presents Darius as an capable, pragmatic ruler under whom the Persian Empire reached its zenith.

Queen Elizabeth: This biography celebrates the long and prosperous reign of Queen Elizabeth I of England. Abbott focuses on Elizabeth's shrewd leadership, religious compromise, and patronage of the arts and literature that fostered English Renaissance culture. The book also highlights Elizabeth's naval defeat of the Spanish Armada which secured England's independence from Europe. Overall, Abbott portrays Elizabeth as a commanding, canny and popular female ruler who strengthened England as a major world power.

Genghis Khan: This book looks at the incredible rise of Temüjin, better known as Genghis Khan. It follows his hardships as an outcast youth to becoming the fearsome founder of the Mongol Empire. Abbott chronicles Genghis Khan's brilliant military tactics and utterly ruthless conquests that allowed the Mongols to dominate much of Asia and Eastern Europe. Overall it paints him as a complex figure--strategic genius but also brutal tyrant.

Hannibal: This biography focuses on the great Carthaginian general Hannibal Barca. It recounts his famous crossing of the Alps with war elephants and invasion of Italy during the Second Punic War against Rome. Abbott details Hannibal's victories in major battles like Cannae but also his eventual defeat by Scipio and exile. The book celebrates Hannibal's daring military prowess but also concession late in life that Rome could not be conquered.

Josephine: This book examines the life of Josephine Bonaparte from her aristocratic upbringing in Martinique to her marriage to Napoleon Bonaparte. It focuses on Josephine's time as Empress consort of France

BIOGRAPHIES ABBOTT WROTE

and her support for arts and education. But it also discusses Napoleon's eventual divorce from her due to dynastic pressures. Overall the book presents Josephine as an intelligent, compassionate woman who tempered some of Napoleon's ambition.

Julius Caesar: This traces Caesar's life from early military campaigns to dictator and eventual assassination. Abbott covers Caesar's conquest of Gaul, rivalry with Pompey, famously crossing the Rubicon and crowning as dictator. The biography also examines the conspiracy led by Brutus and Cassius to assassinate Caesar in order to save the Roman Republic. In all, the book presents Caesar as an unmatched military mind who irrevocably changed the Roman Empire.

Margaret of Anjou: This biography looks at Margaret of Anjou who became queen consort to England's King Henry VI. It focuses on the political intrigue and machinations Margaret became involved in to support her husband's reign during the War of the Roses. Abbott portrays Margaret as a fiercely devoted, cunning woman who backed the Lancastrians against factions like the Yorkists led by Richard Neville. Though she lost power, the book frames her as a dominant figure during the conflict.

Mary, Queen of Scots: This book examines the life of Mary Stuart who became Queen of Scotland as an infant. It follows her tumultuous reign marked by scandals and plots to overthrow her by Protestants. Her Catholicism also put her at odds with England's Elizabeth I. Abbott recounts Mary's forced abdication, escape to England, and eventual execution ordered by Elizabeth for plotting against her. Overall it presents a tragic figure whose life was marked by political and religious turmoil.

Nero: This biography looks at the notorious Roman emperor Nero. It explores his self-indulgent lifestyle and tyrannical rule marked by possible matricide and the brutal execution of Christians. Abbott also examines legends around Nero like his fiddling during the Great Fire of Rome. The book presents a despotic, unstable man who drastically weakened the Roman Empire.

Peter the Great: This book covers the reforms and policies of Peter the Great that rapidly westernized Russia. Abbott discusses Peter's extensive European travels as a youth and later programs to remake Russia's army, expand its naval fleet, and build a new capital in St. Petersburg. The biography also examines Peter's harsh, authoritarian approach to governing that consolidated his power. Overall it presents him as a pivotal, transformative tsar.

Pyrrhus: This examines the life and military exploits of Pyrrhus, king of Epirus. It focuses on his campaigns against Rome where he won major battles but suffered heavy losses, giving rise to the term "Pyrrhic victory." Abbott recounts Pyrrhus's struggles to build a Greek empire and failed invasion of Sicily against Carthage. Though a skilled commander, Pyrrhus ultimately failed to achieve lasting gains.

Richard I: This biography looks at the reign of Richard I, known as Lionheart. It focuses on Richard's leadership during the Third Crusade to recapture Jerusalem from Saladin. Abbott also details the legendary tales of Richard's bravery and valor in campaigns against France and during his imprisonment. Overall, the book presents Richard I as one of England's great warrior kings.

Richard II: This explores the reign and overthrow of King Richard II. Abbott covers Richard's despotic actions that led the nobles to revolt and install Henry IV, leading to Richard's imprisonment and likely murder. The biography presents a weak king whose tyranny and poor leadership during a peasant's revolt cost him power and his life.

Richard III: This delves into the controversial rule of Richard III. Abbott examines Richard's contested path to the throne and the disappearance of the Princes in the Tower which Richard likely ordered. It also portrays Richard's defeat at the hands of Henry Tudor at the Battle of Bosworth Field that ended the Wars of the Roses. Ultimately Abbott paints Richard III as willing to employ any means to gain and retain the English crown.

Romulus: This recounts the Roman legend of Romulus and Remus, twin brothers raised by a she-wolf who went on to found the city of Rome. Abbott covers the myths of the brothers' quarrel over leadership, with Romulus killing Remus and becoming Rome's first king and architect of its nascent political institutions. Though mythological, Romulus represents ancient Rome's founding origins and rise to power.

William the Conqueror: This biography follows William, Duke of Normandy's conquest of England in 1066 after victory at the Battle of Hastings. Abbott discusses William's reign as king where he consolidated control, introduced feudalism, and fused English and Norman culture. William is presented as a formidable, innovative Norman leader who irrevocably transformed Anglo-Saxon England.

Xerxes: This examines the reign of Xerxes I of Persia, known for his failed invasion of Greece. Abbott focuses on Xerxes's gathering of a massive army to crush Greek resistance, but defeat at Salamis ended his ambitions. The book covers later unrest and palace intrigue that clouded the end of Xerxes's reign. Overall he is portrayed as a rash ruler whose desire for conquest led to disaster for Persia.

www.ingramcontent.com/pod-product-compliance
Lightning Source LLC
Chambersburg PA
CBHW070102080526
44586CB00013B/1157